From Manila to Miami: My Journey to a Meaningful and Joyful Jewish Life

From Manila to Miami: My Journey to a Meaningful and Joyful Jewish Life

CONVERSION TO JUDAISM: JEWISH BY CHOICE OR WAS I CHOSEN?

Belen Loreto Grand ARNP

ISBN: 0997155507
ISBN 13: 9780997155501
Library of Congress Control Number: 2017904659
Cosmic Editions LLC., Miami, FL

To the Divine Creator, who gave us life...

To the Rebbe, Menachem Mendel Schneerson, O.B.M., for his spiritual guidance and vision and to the Rebbetzin, Chaya Mushka Schneerson, of Righteous Memory, for her dedication to Chassidim.

To my husband, Robert, for your unconditional love and support.

Table Of Contents

Preface

BEFORE YOU BEGIN, KNOW THAT: I am not an authority in Judaism, I'm a beginner level student of Torah.

I. This is not a theological discussion on spirituality but rather a personal journey of the dilemma and soul-searching that led me to a meaningful and joyful existence following the Jewish faith.

II. To my non- Jewish readers, some of you may have questioned your past and present beliefs but don't know what to do. This book will give you a glimpse of the path I took when I left the religion I was raised, and embraced Judaism. Details of my experiences and the why, who, what and how are disclosed for everyone to peruse.

III. In a lighthearted manner, a few Yiddish and Hebrew terms for some holiday celebrations at Chabad synagogues are defined for all readers to understand.

IV. As a proud JAP (Jewish American Pinay), the historical significance of Jewish presence in the Philippines is discussed in Chapter 17 such as the "**Open Door Policy**" that saved between 1200-2000 European Jews during the Nazi era as well as the significant contribution by Jews in the development of the Philippines' economy, arts, music and dance.

V. The chapter on "Jewish Perspectives" quote valuable insights of rabbis and authors whose work I hope my readers will contemplate upon.

VI. Among Jews who are not involved or say "I'm spiritual but ....." my objective is for you to look at Judaism in a different light and revisit a beautiful way of living with the Torah as the blueprint. Practical tips were included to familiarize everyone to the major holidays and life cycle events celebrated with so much fun and meaning at Chabad synagogues all over the world.

VII. To my Jewish readers, my objective is ***not*** to admonish because that will negate my intentions but I'm delighted if you can cruise with me and relish the personal transformation despite my snail paced but enthusiastic embrace of Judaism.

Belen Loreto Grand
Miami, Florida. April 2017.

CONNECT WITH ME: I LOVE TO BE IN TOUCH WITH MY READERS.

FACEBOOK: BELEN LORETO GRAND
WEBSITE: WWW.COSMICEDITIONS.NET
EMAIL: COSMICEDITIONS@GMAIL.COM

Acknowledgments

FIRST AND FOREMOST, MY GRATITUDE to Hashem for paving the path for me to meet Jews and learn about Judaism.

To the Chabad Lubavitch movement for their dedication in bringing Judaism to all corners of the world.

I extend my heartfelt thanks to the many Chabad rabbis and rebbetzins who along the way showed me how to live as a Jew by opening their homes to my husband and myself for Shabbat, Jewish holidays and many joyous occasions. I can't thank you enough and may you all continue to bring light to this world thru the work you do. (Below is a list of Chabad rabbis and rebbetzins we've had wonderful memories over the years; there were many more who gave us warm welcome in the many trips to Europe and Asia).

Rabbi Nir Donenfeld and family of Chabad of Cebu, Philippines
Rabbi Yacov and Rebbetzin Gutal Fellig of Chabad of Coconut Grove, Florida
Rabbi Mendy and Henchi Fellig of the University of Miami in Coral Gables, Florida

Rabbi Yossi and Rebbetzin Nechama Harlig of Chabad of Kendall and Pinecrest, Florida
Rabbi Zev and Rebbetzin Chani Katz and family of Chabad House in Miami Beach, aka *Chabad House on Wheels* of Miami Beach, Florida
Rabbi Yossi and Rebbetzin Tiferes Levy of Chabad of Manila, Philippines
Rabbi Mendel and Rebbetzin Esther Lifshitz of Chabad of Boise, Idaho
Rabbi Shmuel and Rebbetzin Tzippy Mann and family of Chabad of Venetian Islands, Florida
Rabbi Ephraim and Rebbetzin Nechamy Simon of Chabad of Teaneck, New Jersey (formerly of Chabad of Coconut Grove, Florida)
Rabbi Avrohom and Rebbetzin Chany Stolik and family of Chabad of Downtown Coral Gables, Florida
Rabbi Mendi Sudakevich and family of Chabad of Tokyo, Japan

My special thanks to Rabbi Zev and Rebbetzin Chani Katz and family for the warmth, kindness and compassion you have shown to the community and allowing us to share the many spectacular life cycle simchas and making us feel like members of your extended family. To Mendel, Chaya, Baila, Motty and Miriam Katz, it is a joy to watch you grow up in a loving Jewish home and for sharing your beautiful pictures.

To my Torah and Tea women's group under the guidance and leadership of Rebbetzin Nechama Harlig, thank you for the wisdom and insights shared every Thursday.

To our friends at the Friendship Circle, you've taught us valuable life lessons and have inspired us in so many ways.

To Chana Rosen and Michael Gardner for introducing us to the wonderful world of *CHABAD* .

To my parents who were my first teachers; Cesar Torres Loreto and Enriqueta Santa Iglesia-Loreto (RIP), I cherish your memories. My gratitude to both of you for the faith in G-d and open mind you had instilled in me that allowed me to question my past beliefs and forge my own in my quest to settle my restless soul.

To my brothers and sister, for your understanding (despite your occasional obvious quiet protests which I comprehend), and hopefully your full acceptance of the divergent life and spiritual path I took.

To my very good friend, Elinor Medina Faldas, for being present when you were needed most.

My heartfelt gratitude to the families of David and Jeanine Berman, Michael and Cynthia Gruen, Mendel and Karen Nestlebaum, Dr. Barry and Lisa Eichenbaum, Atty. Alan and Darby Ginsberg, Dr. Alan and Andrea Levitt, Dr. Richard Lapin, Drs. Shirley and William Rappaport, Dr. Lawrence and Stacey Siegel, Dr. Michael Vulfovich, Barry and Ronnie White and our Bagel and Pancit club friends namely; Dr. Mehran & Elizabeth Basiratmand, Jeff and Mercedes Dashesfky, Drs. Divina and Joel Grossman, Dr. Norman and Melanie Levy,

Evelyn and Richard Sussman, Dr. Steven & Lisa Sutnick and Jay and Monette Wasserlauf, thank you for sharing the many holidays and wonderful time spent together with all of you; may we have many more...

PART I

In The Beginning...

CHAPTER 1

Fiddler On The Roof

"YOU'RE FROM THE PHILIPPINES AND you're Jewish...? How did that happen...?Are your parents Jewish...? Did you convert...? When did you convert ...? Are you fluent in Hebrew...?" These are queries I get quite often nowadays....

"It did not happen overnight....but let me tell you my story..."

It has been 40 years since I first saw the Broadway musical, "*Fiddler on the Roof*[1] at the Cultural Center of the Philippines on the suggestion of a cousin who is a Catholic nun. I was mesmerized by this "iconic story of Tevye, the father of five daughters, and his attempts to maintain his Jewish religious and cultural traditions, as outside influences encroach upon the family's lives". This musical moved me at the age of 16; I loved the songs and memorized the lyrics immediately, constantly humming the song of *Tzeite*l and *Motel's* wedding ceremony; "Sunrise, Sunset". Of course it helped that the star of this musical was one of the male heartthrobs, the "Romeo" of Philippine cinema in my generation, Victor "*Cocoy*" Laurel; the American educated son of former Philippine Vice President Salvador Laurel and stage actress Celia-Diaz-Laurel.

This play is still so vivid to me that I could see the backdrop of the blue clouds, reminiscent of the blue Jerusalem sky hovering over the ***chuppah*** (canopy for a Jewish wedding ceremony) at the wedding of one of *Tevye's* daughters. On both of our weddings (secular and post conversion), the lyrics "is this the little boy I carried; is this the little girl at play…" of the song "Sunrise, Sunset" were played twice 10 years apart.

I never knew any Jewish people when living in the Philippines nor did I understand what Judaism is all about. My first encounter of the word *Judeo*, sadly was a reminder during Good Friday prayers in my Catholic church that a "Judeo or Jew " betrayed Jesus Christ (J.C.) hence he was hanged on the cross. Neither did I know that *J. C.* was a JEW himself. My awareness was somehow concealed in those prayer books and that the 12 apostles were members of the Jewish tribe but then again, I was a young naive Catholic girl following the flock of Christianity. The first movie I saw as a child was "The Ten Commandments" as most Christians probably have experienced; yet as a free spirited teenager, I was oblivious to historical facts and perspectives. It was only after studying and learning Judaism especially celebrating the Jewish Holidays that I understood that the *Last Supper* celebrated by the Christian world during the "*Holy Week*" when J.C. and his 12 apostles had their last dinner together was actually the Jewish holiday week of *Passover*. Initially I was astonished that the holy week and Last Supper occurred on the same week until it finally dawned on me the reason why. Judaism uses the lunar calendar whereas Christians use a Julian/ Gregorian calendar, hence, there are slight differences in the actual days of observance of Passover. The Last Supper is permanently celebrated before Friday (Good

Friday), whereas Passover or Pesach[2] is celebrated for 7 days in Israel and 8 days (in the diaspora such as America) and may fall on different days of the week; Hebrew days begin and end at sundown.

According to Rabbi Ismar Schorch[3] of the Jewish Theological Seminary, "these two holidays were destined to coincide. For Christianity, the belief is that the resurrection took place on a Sunday, the First council of Nicaea in 325 determined that Easter should always fall on the first Sunday after the first full moon following the vernal equinox. By the same token, the rabbis understood the verse "you go free on this day, in the month of Aviv" (Exodus 13:4) to restrict Passover to early spring- in a transitional month when the winter rains end and the weather turns mild. The Torah had stipulated that the month in which the exodus from Egypt occurred should mark the start of a new year (Exodus 12:2) the end of the prior year was subject to extension to keep the Jewish lunar calendar in sync with the solar year. Friends and family who ask me are actually starting to acknowledge the connection of these two festivals celebrated by Jews and Christians.

College was spent in Manila and it was at this time that I had started questioning some of the accepted Catholic sacraments of confession and communion as well as the 3 beliefs outlined below. (I subscribe to a personal relationship with G-d but I am not imposing this to anyone, as they say, just the facts please....To my Catholic and Christian family and friends, don't shoot the messenger, instead, kindly open your mind and broaden your horizon or at least finish reading this book, something might resonate to you somehow, I promise...).

a. Original sin- Christians are born sinners
b. Trinity – G-d the Father, G-d the son and G-d the Holy Spirit
c. Non-believers of Jesus Christ will **not be saved** and will go to hell.

Sinner….!!! Me a sinner? Nope, this to me is relative truth. I am an optimistic person hence I defied the notion that I am a born sinner, period! Despite explanations about the original sin and trinity; the obstinate me just doesn't want to carry that guilt. I believe in one supreme creator, one G-d and the oneness of G-d. (Hmm, I prefer direct flights so I wanted direct connection to G-d). Family and friends get exasperated but I rest my case immediately; I refrain from arguing because no one wins in any religious discussion, instead, it will just breed animosity so I let them know that I understand and respect the same belief indoctrinated to me growing up in a Catholic family. I set boundaries and express appreciation of a reciprocal understanding and acceptance; after-all this was my rational choice as a mature adult and aren't we supposed to espouse "Love your neighbor as thyself?"

The *original sin* was incomprehensible and bothered me but I didn't know how to get the right answers. I was just focused to finish my nursing degree and pursue a career, immigrate to America, earn dollars and like most Filipina nurses, send green bucks back home to help my family. (The political and economic instabilities of the 1980's caused a brain drain, prompting an unusual migration of Filipinos to the west in search of a greener pasture).

I have always been astutely sensitive to other people's feelings and in my college Humanities class I actually engaged in a discussion and challenged my professor to explain how my Muslim classmate will go to hell even if she espouses "brotherly love", is kind and loving, if she is a non-believer of J.C. I never got a satisfactory answer, and that left a void in my psyche at that time.

In my youth I always questioned ideas and beliefs embedded in my mind thru generations of association and acceptance of that belief. In the words of my mom I always had an inquisitive and sometimes, radical mind hence she sent me to Manila to avoid being influenced by the notoriety of some left leaning students at the prestigious University of the Philippines in Cebu where I had been admitted. It was a period of awakening for me when the sacraments of confession and communion no longer spoke to me. Nowadays, I am very confident that my personal connection with G-d as a Jew is very personal and vital to my existence such as my daily morning and evening prayers of **Shema,** observing the Sabbath, and the ten commandments and many more.

Every Saturday from 1975-1976, on my way to catch a ***jeepney*** (colorful open –air vehicle commonly seen in Philippine city streets, whose origins were from the recycled surplus US military jeeps after world war II); I occasionally encountered a young man or two with black hat and black suit walking on Saturdays to an ornately fenced building located just a few blocks from my aunt's apartment near Taft Avenue. It was odd to me at that time that with the humidity in Manila these guys were wearing black suits!

My curiosity was put to rest when I spoke with the Rabbi at Beth Yaacov congregation in Manila on my visit in 2008 who showed me the picture of the building (and the $1.00 from the

Rebbe, Menachem Mendel Schneerson, OBM prominently displayed on the bulletin board).That was the old synagogue, built by Emil Bachrach, one of the first and prominent Jews who settled in the Philippines along with the Nertzogs and Frieders[4] in the 1900's.

With a $100.00 pocket money and air fare paid thru PAN-AM (Pan-American Airlines) Fly Now Pay Later Plan, I immigrated to Miami in August, 1982 and continued my Sunday church rituals and Catholic holiday celebrations until that fateful flight in September,1983 on my way to Zurich, Switzerland to visit my sister. I noticed my seatmate in the airplane was a teenage boy of about 13-14 years; dressed in black suit with side curls (**peyas**) who was seriously reading a book with unusual characters (Hebrew) from *right to left (read back to front).* I myself love to read but what impressed me was his dedication to this book which later I understand was the **Chumash** (5 books of Moses). He politely asked if I could exchange his dollar for quarters to use the payphone to call his mother upon our stop-over in New York. We were both travelling alone but this teenage boy had an aura of emotional maturity, independence, sure of himself, dedication to what he was reading & self –reliance that intrigued me. His demeanor reminded me of an award winning photography by Laura Pannack[5], the National Portrait Gallery International Photography awardee in 2014, the John Kobal New Work Award: Portrait of Orthodox Girl in Synagogue; **"Chayla in Shul"** about an 11 year old Orthodox girl, shy but very mature and extremely intelligent.

This seatmate of mine was a teenage boy on the cusp of adolescence and as Ms. Maya Benton[6] wrote in her description of the subject of Ms. Pannack's photography "teenagers nowadays are generally depicted as a complex mixture of confusion, rebellion, inhibition and awkward insecurities" but, this boy or should I say young gentleman; evinced an air of confident composure and studious equanimity and knew who and where he belonged. I can't help pondering and asking myself; who is this kid and who does he represent; how was he raised and what is his family like? His exceptional composure, aplomb, confidence on an international trip and respectful manners intrigued me. I quietly protected him from a distance when we got off the plane. In Zurich, he was met by his mother and a group of bearded men with black hats whom I later learned were Torah observant "*Orthodox*[7] *Jews*" .

While working as a nurse in Miami, I had made friends with Jewish physicians and a few were open to discuss their religion and lifestyle. Some came from very observant background, "*orthodox*" whose grandparents were holocaust survivors. A few were unaffiliated while some called themselves "conservative" or "reform" but one observation we noticed was that they were genuinely respectful to us Filipina nurses, were dedicated professionals and most had exemplary ethics. What impressed me were their pleasant manners, intellectually engaging attitudes on different topics or ideas and they seemed very cultured with somehow a balanced life and discussions of Broadway shows, opera, symphonies, plays and cultural events were common. I admired their humility and gracious bedside manners unlike the *macho* and arrogant attitudes we've experienced with some physicians we worked with. My colleagues and I generally got along with them.

The *orthodox* were picky when we shared our delectable Filipino dishes of **Pancit** (noodle dish), **Lumpia** (Philippine egg rolls) or **Adobo** (chicken or pork marinated with garlic and vinegar) and would not partake of the food but politely drink Coke (it's ***Kosher***[8] you know); even though back then, I did not comprehend their *kosher* dietary restrictions.

My endless curiosity prodded me to learn more about the holocaust and I watched documentaries such as Escape from Sobibor[9] and movies about Dachau, Treblinka and other films. These documentaries of the extermination camps brought me to tears and I was incredulous that a highly educated and cultured European society was so indifferent and callous (subject to another in depth discussion and many books have been written about the holocaust so I will defer the reader to those books).

I had many introductions to Jewish men. A patient of mine who was a benefactor from Mount Sinai Hospital was eager to introduce me to a family friend so I will supposedly be the 20th match that he and his wife had successfully paired but I politely declined. I also cut-off friendship with a Jewish physician and a chiropractor before I left for Los Angeles, California in 1986 in hopes of finding a match with my "kind" (Filipino) but to no avail.

CHAPTER 2

Chanukah Or X-Mas ? - 1989

AFTER A SKI TRIP TO Vermont, I responded to a voicemail message with these fateful words "how was your Xmas holiday?" The guy on the other line was quiet, so I quickly quipped "Oh, did you have a good **Chanukah**[10] then?" He started laughing since I broke the ice and made him comfortable of my limited knowledge of Jewish holidays; the conversation brought him to his admission as being "Jewish".

Two weeks prior to my ski vacation, I met him at a watering hole (my first time in a bar) at the Brickell area in Miami at "Firehouse Four", then, a hot spot for meeting young professionals for Friday night drinks and hors d'oeuvres which remain a melting pot for young professionals nowadays.

My physician supervisor was kind enough to drive me to this much talked about "happening" area to meet potential soul mates as I've pretty much given up on dating, planned to attend graduate school and told him "all men are the same, they don't want commitments, I think my time will be best used to pursue my Ph.D." A Jewish girlfriend who initiated this idea had to fetch a friend at the airport and her friend's flight got delayed so she never made it back to the happy hour to meet Jewish men. "It was just not meant to be", she said.

Robert's friend exclaimed "you again ?" when he saw me with my boss ! It so happened that the week before, I had a chance encounter with Robert's friend Ed, whose door I knocked on; in search of a phone, to call an acquaintance who lived in the same condominium. Now, just remember, this was before cell phones and I had the **"chutzpah"** (Yiddish term for audacity) to knock on a complete stranger's (Ed's) door at 8:30 in the evening. Was this ***bashert***[11] (meant to be) or not? Ed explained to Robert how we met and that paved the way for a great conversation with Robert and we exchanged phone numbers. On my way home, my boss thought Robert seems to be a nice guy, I confirmed; with a caveat "I hope he's not Jewish, maybe he's not because his last name is GRAND, not a typical Jewish last name of Cohen or Goldberg. My boss (from India but whose BFF is Jewish) chuckled and responded "I think he is; a doctor, born in Miami Beach, he must be Jewish".

Decembers, brought me fond memories of family gatherings and the schism inside my thoughts. It became even more intense when I started dating Robert. Chanukah and X-mas at times coincided on the same week. Chanukah is celebrated for 8 days compared to a 1-2 day celebration for the birth of Jesus (some Spanish countries start on the 24th).

X-mas trees did not bother me as much since I did not grow up having those ornaments, instead we had a nativity scene or Belen; whom I am named after, as a décor for the holidays in our house. The *media noche*[12] dinner on the evening of Dec. 24 was extra special due to my Dad's marinated duck stew with pineapples, roasted garlic and liquor that none in our family could duplicate. The duck was fed with only corn and water the week prior to the final day of reckoning then slow cooked for 24 hours hence it was scrumptious, low-fat and ultra- tender, you can actually eat the bones; better than Peking duck! Mello, my brother, considered our family's best cook can't quite replicate it, neither does my sister who puts European flair to her recipes having lived in Austria and Switzerland for decades. I attempted to cook my own version (using *kosher* duck) a few times, but it is always short of the flavor; we admitted, Dad's culinary expertise in the kitchen on this holiday was what was missing in this festive meal. Thankfully I was not a big consumer of pork dishes; just a bit too greasy although occasionally I tasted the crispy pork skin and the delicacy called *chicharon* or pork rinds.

PART II

Let There Be Light...

CHAPTER 3

"Welcome To The Tribe"

"Belle, my husband is furious that the Rabbi told him that being married to a non-Jewish wife, we can't come to the synagogue for services", my Filipina friend lamented that she felt dejected when I saw her at work years ago.

Frankly, initially I was not warmly welcomed to join the *Jewish tribe* when I first approached a rabbi of my interest for conversion to Judaism. The congregants were warm, accommodating and never alienated me but on occasion I felt ignored, and thought there was some type of ethnic favoritism due to me being Asian. To my husband's credit he was determined and initially withheld this seemingly offensive statement until after we've been attending services at the synagogue. Later on I fathomed the reason for "discouraging and unwelcoming" of potential converts because **Judaism doesn't proselytize**; it teaches that the righteous of all nations have a share in the world to come (Talmud Sanhedrin)[13].

You may have heard of the most famous convert, **Ruth**[14], the Moabite princess and the grandmother of King David. I'm sure if you're a convert, Torah study will never end and you will delve further studying her as you expound your knowledge of Judaism.

Ruth is considered a true convert and is acknowledged for her often quoted phrase to Naomi; her mother in-law " *Wherever you go, I will go; wherever you lodge, I will lodge; your people shall be my people, and your G-d my G-d. Where you die, I will die, and there I will be buried. Thus and more may the Lord do to me if anything but death parts me from you*". One of Robert's first gifts to me was "The Book of Ruth" with this loving dedication "May the verses of Ruth provide you with much enjoyment, meaning and inspiration for our future together" signed in Dec. 1992 (before we got married!).

Before I met my husband, I was already an enthusiastic student of Judaism, conversion was never imposed on me prior to our marriage. I chose my new religion thoughtfully, not by coercion and I had already decided to change when old beliefs and traditions indoctrinated to me ceased to be congruent and relevant to my existence as a spiritual human being. I did not defy conventions of the society I grew up with, just to be different but I know it was time for me to follow my conviction. I believed it was the right thing to do two decades ago as it was then, in 1992. I just did not have the chutzpah to make the drastic changes!

In a sermon from 1983, the Rebbe, Menachem Mendel Schneerson, O.B.M.,[14] argued forcefully for a near-complete democratization of spirituality in the Messianic era, following Maimonidean[15] vision (Maimonides- revered head of the Jewish community in Egypt whose ***Mishneh Torah*** carries significant authority as a codification of Talmudic law. Arabic name is Abu Imran Musa bin Maimun bin Ubaidallah al-Qurtabi; court physician to Sultan Saladin) that **"the entire world will serve G-d together"**. The non-Jew's connection to G-d is not mediated by the Jew, nor is it limited to an inferior, veiled emanation, rather the very essence of G-d will be disclosed to both Jews and non-Jews. The observance of the **Seven Noahide laws**[16] that apply to all humanity that G-d sealed a covenant with Noah after the flood will prevail.

I tried for years to fit in, to please everyone and not ruffle the feathers of family and friends in my quest for peace and tranquility but over time, I realized I don't need others to put me in a box, I can bring in the light. I am comforted that as long as I speak the truth and show love and compassion to others; accept and respect our differences with no judgment or malice then we can achieve happiness and fulfillment in our lives. There are so many healing, energy and spiritual gurus who give lectures all over the world such as the Dalai Lama, Tony Robbins, Christie Marie Sheldon and etc. who are spreading light and love to one another and their work make me very optimistic that G-ds emanation is now spreading and will help enlighten the world.

Judaism is passed down through the mother; so if the father is Jewish, but mother is ***not***, that person is not considered a Jew in the Jewish code of Laws. I know this sounds sexist but as Rabbi Aron Moss[17], had explained; ***"Jewishness is not in our DNA. It is in our soul.*** The child is conceived inside the mother's womb, develops inside and is sustained and nourished and is born from the mother. The child's actual body was never a part of her father's body but was a part of her mother. Every child begins as an extension of their mother's body. The soul identity is more directly shaped by the mother than the father. ***Jewishness is passed down by the mother because being Jewish is a spiritual identity, it defines our very being and our very being we get from our mother both in body and soul".***

What to do, what to do? I of course vacillated for several years. Initially, I purchased a few books on Judaism and attended a formal Judaism conversion/ immersion class at the Miami Jewish federation (where we exchanged love stories and late night talks with many other potential Jewish converts and learned to love the song *L'cha Dodi*). But, I was thirsty for more... My husband had a *conservative* Jewish upbringing and there was no doubt in our household of following Judaism. He also knew my sincere desire and boundless quest to search for truth and learn more about Judaism as we agreed before our wedding with *a Reform* rabbi that if G-d willing Hashem blessed us with a future offspring definitely they will be raised Jewish.

For years I enjoyed many Jewish women's classes, devoured books on how to keep a Jewish home; keeping kosher and a plethora of Jewish topics. (Please refer to appendix on recommended books). We had frequent trips to Judaica stores to quench both our thirst for knowledge and curiosity.

One day in 1993, a co-worker asked me to attend a class with a Chabad rabbi in Coconut Grove and at this time there was a discussion of a trip to New York to see the *Rebbe* and receive blessings and $1.00 but the significance of such journey did not resonate to me then (I wished I made that trip!). Instead, we explored synagogues from *reconstructionist to orthodox* and weighed their pros and cons and my soul searching continued.

The warmth, hands on learning, Torah classes and events and especially the joyful holiday celebrations eventually got us hooked on the Chabad movement with their hands- on, outstanding, Jewish educational system. They welcomed *Jews* from any level of observance. The women's classes were superb and they're initiated by a discussion of the lessons derived from the Torah by a guest speaker or by the *Rebbetzin* (rabbi's wife). This is usually followed by activities relevant for the month, be it learning flower arrangement prior to a Jewish holiday such as **TuBsh'vat,** (holiday celebrating the trees), baking **Challah** or desserts for the month of Elul prior to **Rosh Hoshana**[18].

The classes provided Jewish women the opportunity to prepare and embrace their role in a Jewish home, explore their roots, broaden their knowledge of Jewish concepts, learn a new art or craft and enhance camaraderie and mutual support among each other and of course what's a Jewish gathering without food? This form of education is a common sense approach to teach women life skills; how to live extraordinary lives by the purposeful and meaningful use of one's time; provide opportunities to volunteer in different community events, teach us how to become awesome spouses or parents and create balance and harmony in women's lives. These activities were done thru parenting classes such as Mommy and me, sporting events for Dads and sons, hospital visitations performed by teenagers and volunteer activities for young adults with special needs and other after school programs.

We took Tuesday night Torah classes until I spoke with a *Baalei Teshuvah*[19] Chabad rabbi who impressed upon me that the simplest way to start is to read and learn the ***parsha*** which is the weekly Torah portion. (Thanks to Rabbi Ephraim Simon[20] who was then the assistant rabbi at Chabad of Coconut Grove). I thought this was a brilliant idea to gradually immerse myself. However be warned: the more you learn, the thirst for Torah becomes insatiable and you want to read every book you can avail of or follow different rabbis' wisdom.

My husband still has a clear recollection of the bewildered inquiry of Rabbi Jacobs of Glasgow, Scotland after Robert inquired about purchasing the book **"Little Midrash Says[21]"** ***My First Parsha Reader - 5 volumes of the Torah***, recommended for **ages 3-8.** Here's the conversation: The Rabbi asked **"How old are your** children?", Robert responded: "Ahh... (very long pause)**... 56 and 45** " Rabbi : " Oh... pause... Ok...I got it, no problem, well get those books sent to you asap thru my son who lives in Chicago". He had a non- judgmental attitude; we may not be preschoolers as these books were recommended for, but we certainly were ***real beginners***. I'm still learning from the weekly **parsha**, except now, I read the daily breakdown of the *parshah*, attend weekly women's Torah classes and I'm a devotee of the Daily dose of wisdom of Tzvi Freeman, Yanki Tauber's articles on "The Scroll", Chana Weisberg, Rabbi Jacobson, Rabbi Aaron Moss and everything I can read at Chabad.org.

My sincere interest and some say my **neshama** or Jewish soul have brought me to many synagogues in Miami with different levels of observance. I do not consider myself and will never be a source of, nor an expert in Torah or Kabbalah but my voracious appetite to read and learn expanded the breadth of my understanding of Judaism. Yes, I had rejections in my quest to convert and I was screamed at by a rabbi for driving on the second day of a **Yom Tov** or Jewish holiday (only in life/death situation are you allowed to drive but in my enthusiasm, I did not want to miss the **Yizkor** service recited on the second day of Shavuot in memory of ones' parents. Miami's oppressive heat would have aggravated my asthma at that time; but I comprehend the reaction, Moses too lost his cool at the waters of *Meribah*).

Likewise I encountered several personal "drama" in the process of conversion but I had rabbis, rabbi's wives and congregants who welcomed me with wide open arms. After graduation from a conservative synagogue conversion class, my zeal to learn more was unstoppable. I had contemplated of taking weeks of in- depth learning to be a "*Jewish woman*" at a *Bais Chana Yeshiva* in Minnesota, attended a few lectures by Rabbi Zweig in Miami Beach but instead I decided to live like a Jew before I formally converted. (Coincidentally, my conversion in Dec. 2004 was the 12th year after I was gifted the book of Ruth in 1992, I presume it was my ***Bat Mitzvah*** !).

I gained inspiration and wisdom from some of the notable speakers we've heard at Chabad such as Rabbi Mannis Friedman of Minnesota, Rabbi Simon Jacobson, Rabbi Laibl Wolf of Australia; noted defense attorney Alan Dershowitz, and other inspirational speakers. Jewish books and magazines abound in our household and one of my brothers exclaimed that our home is an information overload of Jewish learning and how to keep a Jewish home.

You may ask: how did I manage to understand the services? At our Chabad synagogue the books are written in both English and Hebrew with transliterations. The rabbi and assistants to the rabbi often announce the pages for the congregants to follow. The organization is cognizant of the fact that majority of the attendees including members of the tribe are not observant or orthodox. There is a gradual immersion of the Shabbat services; I became an expert in finding the pages specially some of my favorite songs. *Ein*

Keloheinu anyone? Some prayers are familiar such as the *Aleinu L'shabayach la-adon* song which is the same hymn that a Catholic priest makes in his final blessing with the incense as he moves around to bless everyone after the service.

My conversion is not devoid of controversy; I'll be the first to admit and in this age of "selfies" we dearly value our privacy. I avoid *lashon hara* or gossip and believe that there's a reason G-d reminds us daily of the importance of this mitzvah that even our matriarch Miriam was given a reminder in the form of **tsaraas**. I abhor gossip, would rather devote my time reading or pursuing activities to achieve self- actualization. The lessons of *Parsha Lech Lecha*[22] **"to go out**, to be in a constant state of ascent" is how I spend my time; developing and elevating my inner potential and our surroundings or volunteering my time for projects that improve our society.

I had my share of resentments and disappointments but after reading **Tanya (**foundational work of the Chabad movement, the philosophy and approach to Hasidic mysticism) and learning that for millennia, Jewish tradition has taught that anger reflects lack of faith and is an impediment to peace and harmony, I very.... gradually came back to my senses. We espouse freedom of choice since G-d gave us free will. I was always eccentric, my husband and I follow the beat of a different drummer, think outside the box and don't submit to the herd mentality as most of our friends and acquaintances will attest about us.

There were many baby steps I took and practices I adapted to live as a Jew. Sometimes I felt I had advanced significantly, yet many times I felt inadequate. My husband's support was immeasurable during times when I felt dejected and disappointed with mundane situations, but when I saw his unwavering commitment to Judaism it helped strengthen my resolve to ignore the noise. During this period, Robert woke up early morning on Saturdays to attend Rabbi Zweig's *Shabbat* services at Talmudic University in Miami Beach although it was mostly conducted in Hebrew. He is not an early riser, especially on weekends, but he had the resolve not to let his Judaism fade away. Eventually, I accompanied him a few times (women's section graced by 1or 2 other women and I was struggling to follow the service being Hebrew language deficient). Obviously, we had our share of life's roadblocks; it's a matter of how to make the most of the circumstances. I unearthed many lessons derived from life's upheavals. Controlling anger is a virtue and not a slam dunk for me but thru osmosis with my partner, I deduced that humility (the greatest asset of Moses) and silence sometimes actually resonate louder than spoken words.

There's different strokes for different folks and many congregants attend different synagogues or choose one that float their boat. The choices could be based on the personal connections they have established with the rabbi or rebbetzin or the friendships forged within the community. The knowledge learned, the laughter and life cycle events shared as well as the joyful community activities and holiday celebrations enhance spiritual and social lives of families.

To say "Judaism adds more meaning to our existence" is an understatement. The many programs the Chabad emissaries do such as the Aleph Institute working with prison inmates, HEART (Hebrew Education for At Risk Teens) in Utah that serves a community of young people with behavioral disorders such as drug addiction or eating disorders, Chabad on college campuses, C-Teens and Friendship circle that provide educational and social services for teenagers and young adults with special needs are just a few examples of the relevance and dynamism that Chabad impacts the different communities all over the world.

My interactions with the observant Jewish families with a firm commitment and relationship with G-d, observing their genuine happiness of living as Torah observant Jews and making a difference in their respective communities, the respect that permeates in the family and the memories they create thru life cycle events of bris, candle lighting ceremonies, bar or bat mitzvah, weddings and the myriad Jewish holidays and their unwavering commitment to the values and traditions is admirable despite the difficult challenges they face. Their acquisition of knowledge and values guide and inspire them to internalize the implications of all the divine miracles throughout Jewish history and in their our own personal lives.

In retrospect my 12 years of delay prior to my conversion was because I was not spiritually nor emotionally ready and my soul was still wandering and did not fully connect yet. **To be Jewish is NOT a Right but a Privilege**. I went thru all those feelings of uncertainty, emotional upheavals and soul searching. You have to have the ***will*** to do so, the urgency and emotional readiness to leave behind the traditions and most importantly the customs, culture, mores and religion that you grew up and be wholeheartedly willing to embrace rituals, practices and specially *the way of Life* of a Jew. It has to be part of your "BEING", your consciousness and conscience are congruent with your physical existence as a JEW. It's not because you eat Kosher food, grace Jewish holiday celebrations or go to services in a synagogue but your soul or **neshama** is enveloped by this "*Jewish Being*".

Anyone who has seen the movie *Brooklyn*[23] can relate to Eilis, the main character's dilemma; an immigrant who is torn between time, place and identity. Like Eilis, I'm called back to my roots; several visits to my homeland fixes my longing but home is now a **Jewish home** in America. I have an aversion to women's small town gossips and men's late night drinking sprees were never my cup of tea. I'm cognizant of the rationale for these gatherings. My *spiritual and cultural separation* from my biological family was gradual but inevitable. In exchange I gained **a huge spiritual family and a tribe all over the world!.** The key to an emotionally healthy existence is acceptance of what was; and making substantial steps forward to what will be; with a keen determination to live a purposeful life.

I knew I was finally a member of the tribe when on a visit to Chabad of Barcelona for Sukkot services in 2009, I noticed a tall, dark and handsome guy who looked like he's on leave from the Israeli army, standing discreetly several feet away, in civilian clothes, kibitzing with a pretty young woman yet discreetly guarding the synagogue ready to aim protecting his flock. But when he saw me kissing the *mezuzah*, he took a deep sigh of relief, gave me a smile and a nod, I smiled back and told myself "I am with my people, where they go, I go" as Ruth would have said.

My passion and conviction to be a Jew was present since my youth; I was never a participant of the frenetic frenzy celebrating the biggest gift-giving holiday on earth. Superficiality has no room in a true conversion; it is a process and a very fulfilling transformation . To me Judaism, is ***NOT just a religion or race, people, customs and culture, BUT a WAY* of LIFE with a central role of having a personal relationship with G-D, the creator with the Torah as our guide.** As a Jew, we are tasked with **tikkun olam** and the development of a society that reflects the creator's goodness and perfection thru performance of "**mitzvot**" or good deeds and following his commandments that espouses brotherly love. As Yanki Tauber[24] had stated at Chabad.org, "*Jews have the ability, the right and the duty to make a difference because, and only because- G-d has empowered us to make a difference. A Jew is a fatalist, in the sense that he believes that whatever transpires is the direct result of G-d's will, but he's also an activist: he believes that there is much he can do and must do, and that what he does makes a difference*".

CHAPTER 4

The Opposite Of Love Is Not Hate, It Is Indifference

A JEWISH MAN ONCE ASKED me *"aren't you afraid of the antisemitism thrust on us, why did you have to convert, we are chosen for what? It seems we're chosen to face persecutions and challenges in life"*. I am very proud that I converted and I know that once I did it, there was no turning back. My years of wandering was over, my restless soul has found a home and I hope I can extract the best in me to fulfill G-d's plans for my creation. I am living a joyful and meaningful existence, determined to fulfill my role whatever and wherever G-d leads me.

In Israel on my first visit, we overheard this conversation between an English boy about to have his Bar Mitzvah and his elderly grandparents at the lobby of the King David Hotel " What do you want to become when you grow old?". The boy responded "I just want to be a *Good Jew*". There, in a nutshell is a simple yet profound answer to a question why convert? I was impressed that at the young age of 13, he already had a firm conviction of what he wants to be and *proud to be a Jew.*

At a trip to Jewish New York with my Torah Women's group in October, 2015 to visit the Rebbe's grave or **Ohel** at the World Lubavitch headquarters, the principal at a girls' school mentioned that one of the main educational objectives is " to teach girls and prepare them of their important roles in a Jewish home". The Jewish woman's role is crucial indeed, especially in nurturing and caring for the husband and family and eventually society at large. A woman's nurture empowers a man or her husband to be stronger and allows him to focus on his career, business or means of living that is eventually beneficial to the family and the community.

In the past, I did not give much importance to the role of women; now what a difference it makes when I am more mindful of the significance of preparing kosher meals, making my house a **Jewish** home and supporting my husband in his career is a very rewarding experience. Judaism espouses a genuine compassion for humanity. The Torah's value system is timeless and stable, it has amplified my desires to reach my full potential, to balance life, to express gratitude daily for G-ds blessings, to give back and be confident in knowing that the separation of myself from others because I am following the Jewish faith defines me.

As a Jew, I have a moral obligation and I am committed to show that compassion and brotherly love will thwart darkness and hatred in this era of confusion and seismic shifts to self- centered materialism. The values I learned and uphold being Jewish; though may be different from others, will not define my self-worth. I am part of a cohesive unit connected by the Torah. We answer to a higher authority, it doesn't mean we are better than others, but we are expected to be a moral compass, an influencer and a giver; not an easy task but with the Torah as our guide, we are up to the challenge ...

The author of Night, holocaust survivor and visionary extraordinaire, Eli Wiesel[25], O.B.M., upon receiving the Nobel Prize for literature on Dec. 10,1986 profoundly expressed the peril threatening humankind whose message in the 1980's is even more urgent to be heard today. Here are a few words to ponder from Mr. Wiesel's speech, "there may be times when we are powerless to prevent injustice, but there must never be a time when we fail to protest. We must always take sides. Neutrality helps the oppressor, never the victim. Silence encourages the tormentor, never the tormented". Mr. Wiesel reminds us that even politically momentous dissent always begins with a personal act- with a single voice refusing to be silenced. Despite his horrendous experiences he didn't go out in the streets killing innocent civilians or exploding bombs in public places to avenge the massacre of the Jewish people. He used his pen to ventilate, teach compassion and understanding as his famous quote says it all that "*the opposite of Love is Not Hate but Indifference*". Judaism teaches humanity at its core.

My husband and I were fortunate to have met him personally and was privileged to talk to him in the elevator at the King David Hotel in Jerusalem one holiday of Shavuot which he claimed was his favorite time to visit Israel (no selfies taken, it was pre- I-Phone period). He exuded an aura of statesmanship and humility despite his stature. He was a shining example of morality, emotional resilience and enlightenment despite what he went thru just because he was a Jew.

These profound quotes of the Nobel laureate resonated to me specially during the challenges of the *great recession* which brought out the best and worst in people, ruined friendships and or cemented relationships depending on the personal accounts (double entendre) of parties involved. It was so palpable in the air that the turbulent financial times had destroyed families, businesses and familial cohesiveness; careers exploded; few were immune to unfortunate circumstances. However as we learned from the *parshah* Balak[26] " **every part of creation, even the most negative aspects, can be transformed to good";** as the saying goes, we can make lemonade out of lemons.

While living at the Sunset Harbor area in Miami Beach, acquaintances from down under in the land of Oz sent me an email requesting that I be the chauffer and chaperone for a 4 day trip to pay homage to Mickey at Disney World(TR) in Orlando with *Rosh Hoshana* and *Yom Kippur* as the 2 dates of choice. (Oy vey of all times!). My emails explaining the sacrosanct Jewish Holidays were not part of the equation for my would be guests, I offered that Friday, before the start of *Sabbath* as my only availability for a lunch and South Beach tour; never mind that I had to delegate the final packing to a brother whom I paid to fly from California and another brother and his family took days off to help us in the daunting task of moving out of our place just to accommodate the Aussies.

Unbeknownst to me, I was designated to pay back the "**utang na loob**"; an ingrained Filipino cultural trait for "*reciprocity*" or a way to pay back gratitude, even if that was incurred by another member of an extended member of the clan. I was vilified; apparently "why was I too busy? As a doctor's wife I was supposed to be the official mascot and tourist guide to wine and dine them (which I used to do!). It was a crime I paid dearly in my family relationships (missed a beloved niece' wedding) that plunged me into an abyss that took years for me to extricate from. Was it the dreaded word of anti ___? I may never know...I refuse to hate...let's not go there... Unfortunately....occasionally... we have to deal with the uncomfortable truths in life.

This episode descended like a powerful category 5 hurricane; thankfully my husband's empathy and warm embrace on my early dawn crying spells helped me ride out that perfect storm until G-d eventually sent me a rainbow. *Lashon hara* or gossip and a saga similar to the biblical story of Joseph and his brothers and the subsequent reconciliation was a life- altering wake up call for me (no worries, I will spare you the drama!). A lovely quote from Jacki Whitford, community manager for Christie Marie Sheldon's Love and Above Program[27] is so apropos "their actions are not my responsibility; however I am responsible for my reactions". It was emotionally painful but the Torah guided me to a path in a quest for enlightenment and I dug deep in search for the true meaning of my existence.

A prayer in the Siddur that I fervently recite "Jews should not rely on the hands of man but on G-d alone" was a phrase I reminded myself daily. The word "alone" is so transformative when you are literally and emotionally alone . The profound words of Anne Frank[28] also resonated when she wrote "despite everything, I still believe that people are really good at heart"; my recollection of the climb to the narrow stairs to her secret annex in Amsterdam made me feel like we shared a sisterhood during those tumultuous years of mine.

The sad episodes in my life taught me resilience and self- correction of my ego as well, which could have sent a negative vibration that contributed to that vexatious chapter of my life. My daily practice of connecting with Hashem, meditation on compassion, gratitude and forgiveness are now essential to my being and made me more excited of what the future brings. In retrospect, I was very grateful for the period of self- introspection and soul- searching (this journey would not have been chronicled). The moral values I gained from Torah's life lessons propelled my quest for enlightenment and actualize my potential. Love still permeates in my universe and I made a conscious effort to replace that dark episode to embody a healthy mind and spirit. I resolved that my setback was a set-up for a strong comeback! Sometimes we see ourselves as victim of circumstances yet **it is not necessarily so in actual fact!**

Que sera, sera? What will I be and whom will I marry? A conversation I had with my mother before I immigrated to America went like this "what if I marry a man who is not Catholic?" Her response was "as long as he loves and respects you and believes in G-d", which must have been a premonition then. Many relatives and acquaintances in my original tribe questioned my decision to follow Judaism; some thru subtle gestures of disapproval, others with innuendoes, sending their concern via Facebook and one sent angels to watch over me so I will wake up; another said my mother will roll in her grave. Their assertion and contention, claiming that their religion is the *right one*; accusations of me being **a fake** are all understandable. I can fathom their dilemma; I am realistic that acceptance will take time or may never come but I find solace in following Judaism as my spiritual and rationale choice as a mature adult. I don't need to fit in to everyone's agenda and neither did I make a pact with anyone about my spirituality.

Friends or family members harbored deep resentment that I should have violated the *Sabbath* as an exception for one special occasion that will happen once in their lifetime (you can fill in the blanks... son's graduation, weddings, B-day, baptisms etc.) My response was always with a listening ear, empathic, non-confrontational. Respect and understanding of my religious holidays were all I asked but those quests were elusive then. When I showed my firm conviction of the observance of the Jewish holidays as non-negotiable; then I got accepted and respected but still misunderstood; occasionally I received the same biases from acquaintances of the non-observant Jewish tribe.

That descent in my life certainly was a catalyst for my ascent to create a system of living and patterns that lead me to become a more joyful human being. My life is more important than the opinion others make of me, the dysfunctions we encounter in life teach us to shift our energy to a life of commitment and dedication to a mission greater than ourselves. I am very happy to follow my conviction, I cut emotional chords from different people and allowed a positive energy to influence me. One practical action I did was to provide a Jewish calendar to a member of the family or post on FB(TR) that I will be incommunicado for certain days hence family members become familiar with the significance of the ***Yom Tov*** days and why they are celebrated. Arriving late at Filipino wedding receptions to ensure I don't break the *Sabbath* is a common occurrence nowadays but the difference is that my *Sabbath* observance is now being explained by friends or family members to other attendees at this gatherings. (Voila ! some things are changing...). Not so fast...I still get lots of Merry X-mas greetings. Need I say more?

The Torah taught me to live a more compassionate and peaceful existence and find the meaning of a life well lived and fulfill G-d's master plan of my creation. I denounce racism and as Mr. Wiesel said, "no human race is superior; no religious faith is inferior; all collective judgments are wrong; only racists make them". However, the reality in life is that one will have critics, we can try our best but we can't please everyone and we have to have that willpower to pursue what we believe is best for us.

I forgave myself for feeling being a "victim" of that unpleasant situation, I focus on the positive and I am grateful for being able to work in this country where millions of people risk their lives in search of the much clichéd "American dream" (Siri on my I-phone had been screaming at me to ***recalculate!***).

The star of David shines brightly in my quest to live a Jewish life and is rendering me personal satisfaction and a sense of achievement in my own unique ways. It is humbling to hear Jewish acquaintances happily report to me that they are inspired by my conversion and now light candles on *Shabbat*. A realtor in Asheville, North Carolina a few years ago, sent us a holiday card, breaking the news that Chabad Asheville finally opened after the officers from their synagogue agreed to meet with the Chabad rabbi emboldened by our positive comments about Chabad as an organization during a *Kiddush* lunch we shared with the president of the conservative congregation the prior year.

In this current era, accumulation of material wealth is a measure of success with conspicuous consumption as the new norm. Many individuals have fame and fortune, yet, are malcontent. No amount of materialistic pursuits from Prada(TR) to a Tesla(TR) to yachts and vineyards could satisfy their desires.(I was guilty of this vice as well, in the folly of my early adulthood during the materialistic 1980's, I had a *nouveau riche* mentality. Due to my vast shoe collection then, I was referred as a mini Imelda of Marcos' fame who hailed from my province of Leyte). Most people judge one's success with the size of the house or at what exclusive residential area he/she lives, the car on the driveway or the latest luxury posted on Facebook(TR). Meanwhile I've talked and mingled with people who are living blissful lives among observant Jewish families who are happy and have supportive families. They show genuine love, care and warmth to fellow Jews in their homes during *Shabbos*; some are endowed materially but many are not, but they have found a deep sense of purpose in their existence. I don't despise material wealth, one can flaunt it to his/her heart's content after all, this is a free world.

As a Jew, I commiserate with the Jewish nation who has been dispersed, encountered insurmountable suffering and immense persecution throughout history yet has outlasted ancient civilizations (remember the Romans and the Greeks?) and yet Israel is still the center of major political discussions. Many Jews (including some who even tried to deny their identity) throughout history have mind boggling achievements in the arts, music, literature, science, medicine and technology. The emphasis on education and learning, the Torah as their blue print in life, doesn't surprise me that more than 50 % of Nobel awardees are from the Jewish tribe, yet the indifference, fine needle scrutiny on Jews and Israel, antisemitism and distorted facts by the United Nations is disturbing.(I will defer from delving into political discussions here).

How many countries or a group of people can we count on who have excelled in discoveries from Aspirin to Polio vaccine, Laser, drip irrigation, desalination, water recycling and anti -missile defense batteries despite non- ideal circumstances such as wars from neighboring countries? Have you ever wondered why major tech companies such as Google and Facebook, set up shop in Israel and pursue the talents of Jews despite the instability of the middle east ? An in-depth discussion of this can be extracted from the book *Start Up Nation*.[29]

I have always admired how Israelis and Jewish organizations are generally the first rescuers seen at the scene of disasters and the international community always welcomed their arrival especially during the earthquake in Haiti. Danny Pins, whose mother and grandparents were among the German Jews who fled to the Philippines for safe haven in 1938 led a team of disaster experts from the Jewish Joint Distribution Committee after typhoon Haiyan in the Philippines.[30] They don't expect media publicity, they're there sincerely to provide aid and rescue people because Jews are taught to *love thy fellowman* and are commanded to follow the Ten Commandments given at Mt. Sinai of which the essence is brotherly love.

PART III

The Promised Land...

CHAPTER 5

Shabbat Or Shabbos An "Island In Time"

THOSE WHO OBSERVE IT LOOK forward to it and they savor the experience, sanctity, beauty and peace of this day of rest. To the non-observant, and to some Jewish acquaintances, this is an old tradition, not applicable nor appropriate to modern times, but it is actually what I believe is necessary for "modern" times that frees you from all the gadgets and instant messages in this 24 hour modern era and liberates one from the hectic pace of the rat race. CEOs and CFOs, mothers and everyone can actually relax, contemplate with their creator and have quality and uninterrupted time with their families. I'll tell you why, in my opinion, this is one of the secret weapons of Judaism to keep families intact, preserve traditions and moral values that treasure humanity, live a purposeful existence with a personal relationship with G-d, the source of everything in the center of one's being. As Rabbi Noah Weissberg[31] of Aish Ha Torah stated in a nutshell "***Shabbat** has been the Jewish oasis in time. Once every seven days, we step back from the world and make a statement to ourselves and humanity that we are not in charge of this world. We stop all creative work and acknowledge that it is* **G-d's world, not ours**".

"Remember the Sabbath day, to sanctify it. Six days you may work and perform all your labor, but the seventh day is the Sabbath to G-d, your G-d. You shall perform no labor" is the fourth of the ten commandments, G-d gave to the Israelites from Mount Sinai (Exodus 20:8-10).[32] **Shabbat** is observed a few minutes before sunset on Friday evening until the appearance of 3 stars in the sky on Saturday night. Shabbat is ushered in by girls above 3 years old and women lighting candles and reciting a blessing 18 minutes before sundown on Fridays to welcome the *Shabbat*[33] queen.

At Chabad, we also delight in the tradition of dropping a few coins in the **pushka** (charity box) before Shabbat, practiced in many homes . "Provide for others and G-d will provide for you". Boys and girls or in our home, myself and my husband, enjoy this act of doing **tzedakah** together. Charity giving instilled and observed by children in their early life, hopefully translates to altruism among teens and adults who will genuinely care about the plight of the underprivileged instead of creating this *me only* generation. This weekly habit of putting coins on the charity box eventually develop traits of compassion for the needy so as children become adults they will learn to balance being givers not just as receivers!

Peace be with you ! (Shalom Aleichem) is a traditional song sung every Friday night upon returning home from synagogue prayer, it signals the arrival of the Jewish Sabbath welcoming the angels who accompany a person home on Sabbath evening then **Eishet Chayil** is recited. Many understand this as a song of praise and thanks that family members sing in honor of the matriarch of the home for all that she does during the week and what she has done getting ready for Shabbat. This prayer is a subtle reminder to husbands and children of the importance of mothers in the house and you don't have to nag them to say it ! (Moms, don't you want this adulation too?).

It is indeed a beautiful sight to observe and to be part of the *Shabbat* celebration of orthodox and or *Shabbat* observant families with girls rushing to get into their best dresses and suits for boys, after all the chaos and frenetic energy of preparation, the smell of *matzoh ball* soup simmering in the kitchen, the aroma of freshly baked challah bread wafting in the air and your best dinner of the week be it baked salmon with dill, beef brisket cooked to perfection or baked chicken with lemon and herbs, an array of salads and appetizers and of course delectable desserts.

Creative vegetarian meal is not an exception; *Shabbat* dinner is special. Families will reserve their best food for *Shabbos* and is a perfect time to show off your favorite recipes. Your fine china and cutlery set on top of your best table linens, what a sight to behold! If you have not graced this occasion once, I urge you to ask to be invited or crash into this party and you will have a sense of envy of this weekly Jewish holiday. One gets easily hooked, hence I look forward to it weekly. I have Filipino family and friends who have lined up and want to be invited to this weekly celebration.

My first *Shabbat* dinner invitation was filled with fear of the unexpected, of not knowing how to behave, yet, I was also excited to have dinner with a young Chabad **schluchim** (emissary) in our neighborhood. Upon arrival at the rabbi's house, my husband's gesture to shake hands with a teenage looking *rebbetzin* was rejected. (It was explained to us later that opposite sex doesn't shake hands when one is married). Of course we were astonished but we just went with the flow so don't be offended if this happens to you.

The evening meal started with wine blessing called **kiddush** over kosher wine followed by handwashing with blessings using a pitcher with 2 handles before the ***hamotzeh*** or blessing over 2 loaves of challah was recited (symbolic of the double portion of manna that fell from the sky during Sabbath when Jews were wandering in the desert-a reminder that G-d alone is responsible for our sustenance. (Oh by the way, it is a tradition not to talk after handwashing until after partaking of the bread).

Robert had fond memories of his post graduate years in Tennessee, when *Shabbat* dinners at his friend's relative's home kept him warm during the cold Memphis winters. "My first Sabbath dinner was magical; an experience that left an indelible mark on me. *Shabbat is a spiritual and physical energizer; while the whole world is on fast forward on Friday nights, we Jews are on hold, it is an island in time*". It was at this time that I said, "we should rekindle that tradition, let's make it happen in our home". Words are not enough to describe my feelings of contentment when we bless the wine on Friday evenings and break challah bread (nowadays, mostly home- made with organic ingredients) with friends and family.

I have had several memorable Shabbat experiences and let me indulge on a few of them. On a trip to Paris, we were invited by congregants to join them for Friday *Sabbath* dinner. We walked a few blocks and arrived at an antique building with wide winding stairs and we're welcomed by complete strangers yet connected by this tribal bond. At the dinner table, we were elated to share stories and sang Hebrew songs together. We had an awesome dairy dinner with baked salmon and French pastries for dessert with the family; at the same time I helped relieve the gastric pain of the host's wife who had recently delivered a baby. We walked home with a new Jewish acquaintance. It was past midnight and we couldn't take a cab since it was Shabbat yet, we appreciated the ethereal magic of Paris as the stillness of the night magnified the grandeur and elegance of the city's ornate Gothic and Romanesque architecture as we strolled the streets and acknowledged why the city of lights is still a favorite among honeymooners (including us).

We've had ***Shabbaton*** or Sabbath communal dinners in a hotel at Chabad of Hongkong, and different Chabad synagogues in America such as Boise, Idaho and of course here in Miami. The Chabad of Miami Beach regularly hosts *Shabbaton* for Young Professionals and we're a regular fixture. Rabbi Zev and Rebbetzin Chani Katz once sent us a care package of matzo ball soup, freshly baked challah and a chicken dish when they found out that I severely sprained my ankle and was on crutches after my vacation in the Philippines that had prevented us from gracing these occasions. That's just one of the many gestures of kindness and care we are showered by many Chabad emissaries all over the world. We are one huge family and you can feel the genuine concern for fellow Jews in their respective community.

On a cold December night in 2003 we attended an impromptu Shabbat dinner at the proprietors of the Pita Loca(TR) restaurant at their studio apartment in South Beach. Both brothers immigrated from Israel and are known to be warm and famously invite Jewish tourists and their customers for Shabbat dinners. There were about 75 guests seated on one elongated table of approximately 3 ft. x 50 ft. and we were shoulder to shoulder with each other but we seemed to fit except we all had to stand when one needed a bathroom break. All the guests were just passing by Miami, either going or disembarking from cruise ships, or flying to different destinations. The cacophony of conversations and laughter filled the miniscule room, somehow we managed to get to know our seatmates who were from California, Colombia & Israel. It ended with Israelis singing Hebrew songs and Shabbat melodies while we had great camaraderie. Where else can you find strangers becoming friends overnight because of this tribal bond? Can you tell me where? That's unique to the Jewish tribe!

Our attempts to attend Shabbat services while on a trip to Avignon, France in 1996 had a few interesting twists. The message we left of our plans to visit the synagogue for Friday evening services was not answered but we were not deterred. Upon arrival, we saw a huge sign at the door that stated "*please be aware that security is strictly enforced*" and noticed surveillance cameras in the premises. Most synagogues in America don't have as tight a security system as Europe hence we took it in stride. No one came to greet us, we did not want to overwhelm the congregants so we got out quickly and lo and behold a police car with 2 burly police officers interrogated us outside. Thankfully, we seemed credible and one of the security men instead related his nostalgia of his visit to South Beach and they apologized that they can't allow us to go inside due to security protocols.

Our obstinacy brought us back the following morning hoping to meet someone outside who will usher us in -but no one was outside; instead on that chilly October morning we saw the same police car passing by and waved to us; at this point we decided not to try our luck one more time. We left disappointed but along the way I saw my favorite red striped pashmina wool scarf that I lost in our rush the day before, wrapped around the neck of a beggar on the street parallel to the synagogue. I thought he needed it more than me since it kept him warm and he was happily singing so I decided that it was my donation.(As a Floridian, temperatures below 60 degrees is winter for me). In Europe, synagogue security is taken seriously so beware to avoid embarrassment. Early and proper communication is a must. We had successful visits in Zurich, Barcelona and Italy after sending early email messages; in fact, we had VIP seats with our names printed on our visit to Florence, Italy on ***Rosh Hoshanah*** (Jewish New Year) a few years ago.

Sabbath dinners at home were coveted invitations among colleagues and friends both Jews and gentiles. Previous guests still remember when I see them around in Miami. Even the excitement of using regularly your fine china and silverware is a nice ritual, instead of bringing them out once or twice a year only. A co-worker was adamant to get the *Bartenura*(TR) *kosher* wine to give as a gift since she couldn't stop raving how good it was. (On Shabbat, everything tastes spectacular). Shabbat opens communication to different cultures; we had Muslims, Christians and Jews together on Shabbat. It bridges cultural, religious and generational gaps; with food and wine plus desserts, how can we not talk?

Years ago December 31 fell on a Friday, my husband and I decided to host a *Shabbat* dinner on New Year's eve. Our condominium had un-obstructed view of Biscayne Bay with a vantage point overlooking the Venetian causeway in Miami Beach that provided a spectacular 360 degree panorama of the fireworks displayed from Bayside, to Miami Arena. We stayed until the wee hours; no one felt denied by the New Year's fun and fireworks and everyone had a blast on our *Shabbat* table.

Creativity and resourcefulness can be incorporated to make Shabbat experience joyful and memorable. Is it restrictive? Not to me, the *Shabbat* preparations polish my ingenuity and enhances my anticipatory skills since I can't cook on Saturdays. Families united at the table strengthens familial ties. It also sharpens the chef's culinary prowess and is actually liberating when you refrain from talking about work or business on Shabbos. I read an interview of a highly sought after Jewish physician and university professor who was asked "when do you have the time to rest?" and predictably his response was "thank G-d I observe the Sabbath."

As a liver and GI organ transplant coordinator from 2003-2005, my 4 day work week gave me ample time on my Fridays off to prepare for Sabbath. I informed my non-Jewish co-workers the importance of the 25 hour rest period. I was on duty Sundays, Christmas and non- Jewish Holidays; symbiosis worked and everyone was happy. Later, as an Oncology Advanced Registered Nurse Practitioner (ARNP), me and the observant physician I worked with (who has since moved to Tel- Aviv) were focused and superefficient on Fridays since we knew we had to leave work early and mind you this was before Red Bull(TR). In a life threatening situation, one can work on Sabbath since Jewish laws allows us to save lives. A transplant surgeon I had the pleasure of working with actually made rounds at 6 Am on Saturdays when he was on-call before he went to the temple for the ***minyan*** (gathering of 10 post bar mitzvah age, a prerequisite before a Torah can be opened).

Respect is earned when you are committed to something and mean it, in my past career as a research coordinator, my request for an early departure from work on Fridays during my interview was granted upon my job acceptance. In fact my supervisor & colleagues always reminded me when I worked fervently past 4:00 pm; they knew I was not making alibis to attend early happy hour soirees (thanks, Jasmine, Karen and Kamara).

On our visit to Chabad Tokyo, we had an old, blurry aerial print- out of the Chabad house in Japanese, (pre Google and GPS). Thankfully a hotel concierge guided us hence we found the *shul* and we were warmly welcomed by the rabbi and his wife who hailed from Chicago. I helped in peeling carrots and preparing more salads to accommodate the growing congregants who were not expected that Shabbat. We also met the cantor who came from Afghanistan and an eclectic mix of people which made our Shabbat experience even more colorful. Sadly we learned of the incident of the massacre of the Chabad rabbi and his family in India thru email from Chabad of Japan hours ahead of North America.

Our longest walk was in search of the Chabad house in Boise, Idaho.(Yes, there are many Jews in Idaho!). The day before, we had rented a bike and to our amazement; the bike shop was near the *shul* and the proprietor gave us instructions and pointed us to the right way. Hashem seems to always watch over us when we needed directions. The hike was much longer (about 3 hours one way), but that was one of our favorite Shabbos strolls. We savored the scent of wild flowers and listened to the peaceful trickling sound of the water filling our senses. It was very contemplative and refreshing to feel pure fresh air touching our cheeks, gazing at butterflies lilting from flowers to wild berries, listening to birds humming and taking our mini Shabbos nap on benches along the Boise river. Upon our return we discovered a memorial dedicated to eradicating hatred and indifference with quotes from the diary of Anne Frank. Traversing along the winding waterways that the city converted into the Boise River Greenbelt was a sight to behold. Watching families kayaking, children swimming, college students bicycling and canoeing made this walk a memorable one.

There is the thrill of discovery when you take time to look at your surroundings without being encumbered by other thoughts. Happiness can ensue with simple pleasures; appreciating G-d's creations; as the old adage says "smelling the scent of the roses; enjoying the stillness of NOW and precious moments…". Shabbos walk does that to you.

Lighting Shabbos candle is a **mitzvah** (obligation) for Jewish women. Chabad has a custom of celebrating a girl's first lighting ceremony at the age of three. It is a family tradition that girls and mothers join in a special bond. What a privilege it truly is, to light up the dark to make the world bright with Jewish girls' holy spark according to an invitation I got for this occasion. Every *mitzvah* performed strengthens the Jewish nation! Now, if you're a Mom, wouldn't you want to start this tradition with your daughter at an early age as well? Think about it, a weekly tradition that bonds you with your daughters; clothes shopping or a trip to the mall need not be your only way of connecting. Putting coins on the ***pushka*** or charity box will also train daughters to be considerate of the less endowed.

Shabbat dinners usher an open intergenerational communication and allows parents and children to share their achievements and challenges that week. An average American family only have a few minutes to talk to each other due to hectic schedules. Before sundown on Friday evenings, children are encouraged to participate in setting up the tables or those mature enough; to cooking or meal preparation. Parents talk to the young ones and are shown real love and appreciation. The importance of parental bonding affects children at the emotional level. It has been documented that children with close family bonds are less prone to do drugs, alcohol or other illegal activities in their teenage years or adulthood.

On a visit to relatives in Lakewood, New Jersey (a very orthodox **or frum)** community, I thought I was doing a good deed by picking up the newspaper in front of the house. Thankfully, I was not scolded but told in a very nice, softly spoken way that on Shabbos they don't pick up the paper since it will be considered work. It's also a good idea to have Kleenex tissue paper in the bathrooms if one has Torah- observant guest so they don't have to rip off the toilet paper which is not allowed during Sabbath.

The Jewish custom of the father blessing the children on *Shabbat* is so beautiful and touching. This tradition derived from the biblical story when Jacob laying on his deathbed, summoned Joseph in order to bless him; Joseph entered with his two sons Ephraim and Manasseh. The father places his hands on the children's heads and bless them. If there are memories that last a lifetime, a parent's blessing is surely one of them and this is a unique gift that I'm sure kids will remember for generations as well. I often wonder how this tradition would have influenced my brothers and their children if we were born Jewish, would they continue the same ritual to their children, would they feel the power of traditions and feel the strength of generations?

We first realized the importance of **Havdalah** (Hebrew for separation) while on a visit to my husband's aunt in Lakewood, New Jersey. It is a ritual that takes place at the end of S*habbat.* Just as candles are lit to welcome the *Sabbath* on Friday evenings, *Havdalah* marks the end of Shabbat and separates it from the regular weekdays. Wine, fragrant spices and H*avdalah* candles are important components of this ritual. Over-flowing wine symbolizes the wish for the blessings of Shabbat to overflow into the coming week and for prosperity. The smell of spices is meant to revive us as the extra soul that makes us especially attuned to the spiritual world when *Shabbat* departs. The candle's flame symbolizes the *separation between the spiritual and the material world.* It also represents the first light of Creation, renewed energy for the upcoming week and new beginnings. Our awareness of this ritual happened 2 years after we started lighting Friday night candles; we didn't feel inadequate; as we grew in our observance we learned more rituals and fast days to observe as well.

Shabbat comes, Shabbat delights then Shabbat leaves and yet… every Friday night my husband and I look forward to this special day of rest, of peace and tranquility; a spiritual link to Jews all over the world celebrating the significance of this night with a festive meal to share with family and friends and welcome the *Shabbat bride.*

Images

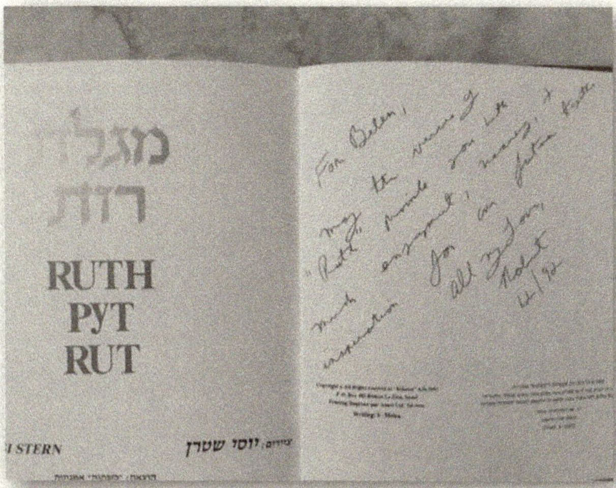

The Book of Ruth with Robert's dedication penned in Dec. 1992, 12 years before my conversion in December, 2004.

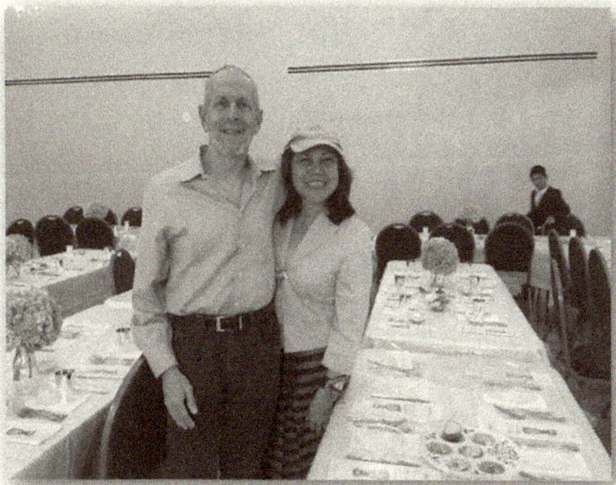

Passover preparation in full swing at Chabad Miami Beach, Florida with then 11 year old Mendel Katz in the background, helping set-up the table.

Chanukah celebration, background is Roger Abramson's shell Menorah at Lincoln Road in Miami Beach, Florida.

Sukkot holiday October, 2015.

Taken after the women's Torah class and dinner with my JAP friends (Jewish American Pinay). (L-R) Monette Wasserlauf, Rebbetzin Chani Katz of Chabad synagogue of Miami Beach, Florida; Belen Grand and Evelyn Sussman.

Challah bread baking during one of our Jewish women's classes at Chabad synagogue of Miami Beach with friends Michelle and Monette Wasserlauf.

Invitation for the first candle lighting ceremony of Miriam Katz at the age of 3.

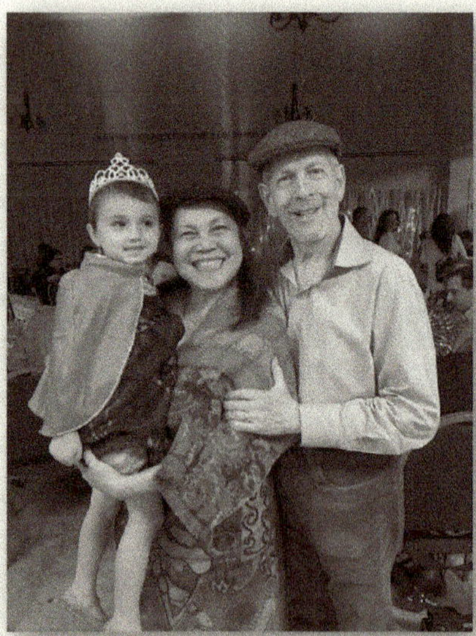

Purim holiday celebration with (Queen Esther) Miriam Katz taken on March 22, 2017.

Of course it's Purim at Chabad synagogue of Miami Beach, Florida

Farbrengen during the holiday of TuB'Shevat with Torah and Tea Women's group from Chabad of Kendall under the leadership of Rebbetzin Nechama Harlig.

At the gravesite of Rebbetzin Chaya Mushka Schneerson of righteous memory.

Trip to the Ohel of the Rebbe, Menachem M. Schneerson O.B. M. in October, 2015.

Motti Katz just finished praying during Sukkot holiday. Miami Beach, Florida

Baila, Chaya and Miriam Katz during Shabbat preparation, Nov. 2015

At the kosher king of Miami; Zak the Baker restaurant & bakery in Wynwood, Florida

Attending a Shabbat dinner at Chabad synagogue of Miami Beach, Florida

My home- baked Challah bread made fresh on Fridays.

With our friends; Dr. Mehran Basiratmand
and Drs. Joel and Divina Grossman

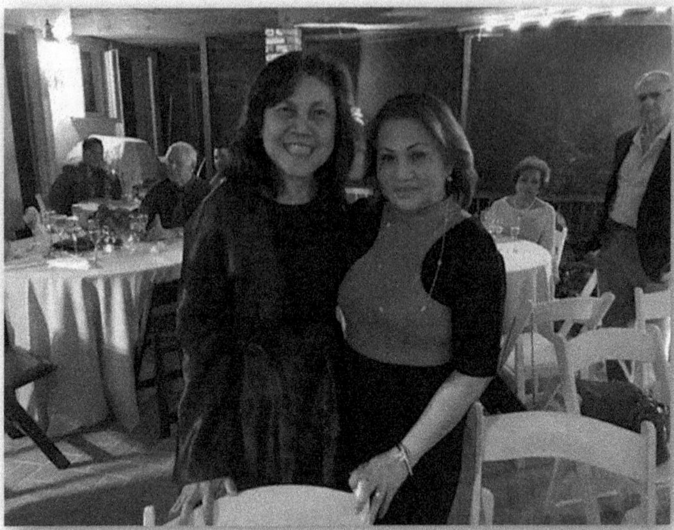

With my other J.A.P. friend, Elizabeth Basiratmand at the engagement party of the Grossmans' daughter.

With IsraAid agronomist and staff. Ormoc city, Philippines taken in April, 2015.

Lance Loreto's first Shabbat dinner (notice his *kippah*). With my niece, Marianne Christelle and sister in- law, Lu Loreto.

As volunteers during the Holidays in Dec. 2015 with friends.

At Mendel Katz' Bar Mitzvah in Miami Beach, Florida

With Baila, Chaya and Miriam Katz at their
brother, Mendel's Bar Mitzvah.

8th night of Chanukah at our home taken in December, 2016.

The oldest and one of the most beautiful synagogues
in America is in Savannah, GA.

Kadoorie Mekor Haim synagogue of Porto, Portugal. Taken in Nov. 2016

Wasserlauf- Knoll wedding under the **Chuppah**. December 11, 2016.

CHAPTER 6

" Wear It With Pride"

MY HUSBAND'S FIRST "TZITZIT" A specially knotted ritual fringes, or tassels, worn by Jewish men as an undergarment; a reminder of the 613 ***mitzvot*** or commandments in the Torah was personally handmade by his orthodox cousin (thanks, Micah) attending a Yeshiva when Robert broached the topic of wearing it. His other cousin (Gavriel) wrote "WEAR it with PRIDE" when we received the package and we were very much moved by his cousin's letter; since then Robert wears it with **Jewish** pride !

On the other hand, around this period, Robert's mother was getting a bit uncomfortable with our regular attendance to activities at Chabad that she actually said "I hope Robert is not going to wear a long beard and side curls (**peyas**)." I'm sure when she first met me, the thought of Belle, a **goy** (neutral Yiddish-Hebrew term for a non-Jew) becoming a potential daughter in- law, must have been difficult for her to fathom and surely had caused tension in our relationship. (Jewish mother – in laws, be careful what you wish for). Some of our Jewish friends couldn't comprehend us not going out to dinner on Friday evenings, it behooved them that we stopped cheering the Miami Hurricanes of the University of Miami football team on Saturdays; I had 50 % discount and had to give away coveted Florida State University vs. University of Miami games.

Certain things in life cannot be rushed, we needed time to savor the process and to me *the journey matters as much as the destination.* Upon learning of my intention to convert, the topic of performing ***tefilin*** daily except on Shabbat & holidays was mentioned by one of the rabbis. (***tefilin-*** two small black boxes with black straps attached to them; putting on *tefilin* is one of the most important *mitzvot* of the Torah). My husband was not ready at all and protested "Oh no, I don't think I can do that, the last time I wrapped *tefilin* regularly was during my Bar Mitzvah; (when he was 13 years old, decades ago); that will take me an hour and I can't even figure out how to tie the knots, how much more doing it daily".

Let's be honest, the word disappointed was an understatement, I muttered "can't he just do it for me?, he should just embrace it for my sake" but, I kept my mouth shut, just empathized with how he felt and patiently waited (unusual for me, I didn't have Zen like qualities then) until he's ready to do it. I thought "will he do it; can he do it ?" I can't coerce him, it has to be his WILL to do it and you can't nag someone to perform this mitzvah.

Our relationship was not devoid of hurdles and it became even more colorful with my interest to convert. Later, I noticed my husband asking the rabbi; yeshiva students or observant congregants to review how to put on *tefilin* properly, performing *tefilin* occasionally at home (slowly with difficulty), making inquiries where to purchase, costs and other details. Then, prior to our second trip to Paris, he broached the idea of buying a new *tefilin* as a special gift to himself since we had our honeymoon there. (FYI: they are not inexpensive; prices vary according to the different leather qualities but the most important is to ensure that it's *kosher* and that Hebrew letters are intact).

Nowadays, his *tefilin* bag is the most important object he will check to ensure our luggage has enough room so it is always with us. I love watching him doing his prayers daily and he relishes this 30 minutes of contemplation which he considers his private moment with G-d. When one has the will, one finds a way to do it and I'm ecstatic that he embraces this ritual and *mitzvot* passionately at his own pace.

CHAPTER 7

Bar And Bat Mitzvah - "Welcome To Adulthood"

PARDON MY PAST IGNORANCE, I did not know that a girl's coming of age at 12 is called **Bat mitzvah,** I thought both are called **Bar mitzvah,** (I wander how many times I've sent **Bar** Mitzvah cards to the girls ?). **Bat** means daughter; **Bar** means son; ***mitzvah*** are commandments or literally to do a good deed.

I have graced many coming of age celebrations such as sweet sixteen and quinces for Hispanics and secular as well as orthodox Jews' Bar and Bat Mitzvah celebrations; I've seen the contrasts of what are important to the celebrants and their families.

The Godly soul enters a woman in its entirety at the age of 12 and the girl attains her religious maturity and becomes responsible to fulfill all Torah commandments. In Judaism, *Bas mitzvah* marks a significant moment in one's life, for a girl, it is reaching a milestone –turning into ***a woman***. As a ***Bas mitzvah***, she makes an eternal commitment to follow the beautiful tradition of Jewish matriarchs (Sarah, Rebecca and Leah) to serve the One Above. It is incumbent upon these *Bas Mitzvah* to live an example of a daughter of Israel. The three mitzvot of Jewish women are: ***kneading and making of Challah, Family Purity or Niddah and Hadlokat Haneirot or the lighting of Shabbos Candles on Friday night.*** *Prior to candle lighting girls put Tzedakah (money for charity to help the needy live).* Now as a Bat-Mitzvah, the woman can have a true experience of fulfilling the commandments as a full participant in this mitzvah-system.

A boy celebrates **Bar mitzvah** at 13 years (boys mature a little later you know, I'm not trying to be biased but it's in the Torah!). Fulfilling a *mitzvah* is obeying a command. It is an act of obedience to a higher authority; **"G-d".** In its deepest sense, ***mitzvah*** - means connection or bond. The human spirit has a transcendent dynamic; the soul wants to connect with G-d. How? By doing a *mitzvah.* Each *mitzvah* is another bridge to the creator, a connection with the divine. After attending a few of these celebrations, I realized that it's not all about food, party and gifts but, that the essence of this Jewish lifecycle event is **to do a good deed**. To be a *Jew is to be actively involved* in*doing good things, and they must result from good thoughts and words* but that **action or mitzvot is what counts.**

"You'll be my guest of honor" exclaimed Robert's cousin when he gave us the invitation to his *Bar mitzvah* when he turned 13. It was a momentous event to witness his cousin whom Robert first met and cradled at the age of 1; I met him when he was a very active but sweet 2 year old boy in New Jersey. The famous lyrics from the song "*Sunrise, Sunset*" from *Fiddler on the Roof* "when did he grow to be so tall, wasn't it yesterday when they were small" are fitting words to describe when you witness the changes both physically and emotionally as a boy matures into a *man* to do the commandments as a **Bar Mitzvah.**

One of the highlights of the ceremony is reading the **Haftorah**. (series of selections from the books of Nevi'im or Prophets that follows the Torah reading of that portion which is sung in a chant). This ceremony formally and publicly marks the assumption of the obligation to take part in leading religious services, to be counted in a ***minyan*** which is the minimum number of people required to perform certain religious services and to make ***aliyah***. As Mendel, the *Bar mitzvah* boy who was the star of Oprah Winfrey's show, "*Belief*" [34] in Oct. 2015; at *Bar mitzvah* " *you say bye-bye to childhood, you think differently and act independently*".

We've seen these profound transformation in Mendel Katz, the son of Rabbi Zev and R. Chani Katz whom we have known since he was an active, playful 3 year old and how the guidance and discipline of his parents provided him the strong foundation of good values and ethics to become an adult. It was so refreshing to receive a thank you card with a letter of gratitude from Mendel for the Bar mitzvah gift and I was doubly impressed that he had shared some of his Bar mitzvah gift to buy a *Tefilin* for a congregant whom he observed has been gradually performing this mitzvah regularly at our synagogue. That is compassion from a young 13 year old boy where Torah teaching and values are unfolding before our eyes, manifested into action without coercion from the parents.

The three girls and other boy (ages 4-8) are already starting to help their mother set up the tables for Shabbat and bring dishes from the kitchen and help in simple tasks in the shul. The girls enthusiastically light Shabbat candles and the boys accompany their father to services. I am not a parent but it is so reassuring to witness that these beautiful Jewish traditions and way of living will be sustained and conveyed towards the future x, y & z generations.

I particularly enjoy the part when family or close friends are called to light the candles which to me strengthen familial bonds. Recently, my coworker excitedly showed me the pictures of his son and daughter who were called to light one of the candles for their cousin's bar mitzvah and that simple act alone is a life- long memory cherished by families. Orthodox receptions for this coming of age Jewish tradition is an all- night affair; men dance with men (and boy can they dance & are really raucous) women to women dancing is mild compared to the men's side. During dinner, both sexes don't mingle so it could be intimidating if it is your first time to attend an orthodox gathering, but in time you'll get used to it, after-all it's a perfect time to be away from your partner for a few hours!

Boys generally prepare with excitement; (parents prepare emotionally and financially, if you know what I mean) mostly for a year, they study with the cantor or the rabbi. Life lessons fitting to a boy's personality or interests are inculcated such as the importance of perseverance or selflessness as virtues important to emulate and were emphatically discussed by the rabbi to our friend's son who is a talented budding artist on another Bar Mitzvah we had attended.

Bar mitzvah and its message is so powerful because this occasion affirms that the Jewish blueprint for living, the teaching of the ***Torah*** will be entrusted now to the next generation. I also witnessed the **talit** (large prayer shawl used by men) handed down from the grandfather of the Bar Mitzvah boy for this occasion in a Reform synagogue Bar Mitzvah. It is a heartwarming sight, profound and overwhelming when you witness the significance of traditions handed down from generation to generation. It is an important coming of age ritual, tears will roll down your cheeks. Jews are small in number, vulnerable in so many ways but the observance of this religious ritual will carry the torch of Judaism to the next generation that despite efforts to annihilate Jews in history, this religious tradition lives on.

CHAPTER 8

The Rebbe's Army

I OWE GRATITUDE TO THE Rebbe, Menachem Mendel Schneersom O.B.M. for inspiring Chabad emissaries to spread **Yidishkeit** and bring Jews back to Judaism to all corners of the globe. The incredible work they do in igniting and enhancing the spiritual growth of Jewish communities throughout the world have awakened the Jewish slumber. In our travels to Asia and Europe, I've noticed common themes of a non- judgmental attitude, warmth and of course their much sought after joyful holiday celebrations have impacted Jews and non-Jews all over the world .Their boundless energy is infectious and their genuine concern for Jews in even the farthest corners is evident in the work they are doing. Bringing Judaism Outward[35] is so appropriate as the title of Rabbi Miller's book since the Rebbe's vision has impacted the Jewish and general society tremendously, so I say why not? The world is ready to know about the wisdom of the Torah.

Some Chabad rabbis hold classes on Noahide laws for gentiles such as Rabbi Levy of Manila and Rabbi Nir Donenfeld of Cebu both in the Philippines. They make their outreach so relevant to the communities they are serving. Another example is Chabad of Rural and Regional Australia or RARA has a bright maroon and yellow motor home or "mitzvah tank" whose rabbi travels 13 hour trips from Melbourne to find Jews in the Australian outback .

Their equally ebullient and knowledgeable wives **(rebbetzins**) are dynamic, brilliant, fashionable and most are very effective public speakers and superb chefs! I am in awe watching them manage their households, raise several young brood and not missing a beat. To observe them before Shabbos you would think that they took Stephen Covey's master classes of the *Seven Habits of Highly Effective People*(TR) because of their laser sharp focus. When you read their articles on Chabad Lubavitch International or Chabad.org you would think these women have doctoral degrees from prestigious Ivy league schools!

Chabad ingenuity and dynamism is evident in the social activities that they engage Jews from different age groups. They are so relevant and technologically savvy, yet deeply rooted in Jewish traditions and are full of passion to light a spark of Yiddishkeit among Jews all over the world. Their outreach for the young professionals such as the "*Holy hour, Happy hour*" on Friday night Shabbat dinners, *BLT or bagel, lox and tefilin* or holding *Kosher food and wine* festivals around the annual Food and Wine festival in South Beach are so culturally contemporary, joyful and effective. Their gestures of kindness and warm embrace of fellow Jews from different levels of observance, the love and appropriate setting of boundaries on their children and the sincerity they exude are ways of living that I admire.

On Lincoln Road, Rabbi Zev Katz and the **bochurim** (students in a Talmudic academy) of Chabad on Wheels in Miami

Beach provide opportunities for Jews to perform the mitzvah of donning **tefilin.** During Chanukah they provide *shabbat* candles to tourists from all over the world. I thought it was a delightful and ingenious act when the rabbi and his team from the **mitzvah** tank happily assisted putting *Tefilin* on Jewish men near the American Airlines arena when our own Miami Heat basketball team was competing in the finals of the NBA years ago. (Alright, we definitely had help from both above and below as we got the championship ring with the other worldly king of the hoops at the helm; Lebron James and the pride of the *Pinoys*; Filipino-American coach, Erik Spoelstra).

Nanotech Engineers decode Talmudic Texts at Rohr Chabad Jewish Center in Albany, New York and at the University of California (UCLA), a significant segment of Jewish students have been drawn into the anti- Israel momentum; yet Chabad's message is "even if we don't agree with your views you are welcome at our *shabbat* table". Chabad makes it a vital part to focus on a Jew's sense of belonging to the Jewish people, strengthen students' identity, engage and help them embrace the true beauty of Judaism.

My husband and I eagerly anticipate the next issue of Lubavitch international magazine with current updates of the activities of different Chabad centers through-out the world. We feel the excitement of Jewish lives in the university campuses, empathize with the emissaries of the challenges they face and how they overcome the hurdles of living as observant Jews without compromising their age-old traditions and moral values.

The Rebbe, Menachem Mendel Schneerson O.B.M. who assumed leadership of Chabad in 1951 opted for inclusiveness and was very progressive and creative in his role and adopted Maimonides' *view that redemption would occur within history and be heralded by political regimes and their constituents embracing monotheism and Torah Principles.* As you can see, political regimes are changing however you perceive it, whether it's the Arab spring turning into a winter solstice or our snail mails now arriving in Cuba from Miami, which is only 90 miles away but due to geopolitical differences, took 50 plus years to be finally received in Havana .

From 1983 to 1987 the Rebbe spoke consistently about the need to vigorously disseminate Jewish values to the broader culture, following the framework of the Seven Universal Laws of Noah. The **seven *Noahide laws*** are the following:

1. Acknowledge that there is only one G-d who is infinite and supreme above all things.
2. Respect the creator- Do not curse G-d.
3. Respect human life- Do not murder.
4. Respect the institution of marriage – Do not be sexually immoral.
5. Respect the rights and property of others- Be honest in all your business dealings.
6. Respect G-d's creatures- Be compassionate.
7. Maintain Justice- Set up courts and bring offenders to justice. We are given the necessary laws and enforce them when necessary.

"There will come a time that the children of Noah will be prepared to return to this path. That will be the beginning of a new world, a world of wisdom and peace. At the heart of this universal code, is the acknowledgment that morality- indeed, civilization itself must be predicated on the belief in G-d. Unless one recognizes a Higher Power to whom we are responsible and who observes and knows our actions, we will NOT transcend the selfishness of our character and subjectivity of our intellect". (Miller, Chaim: *The Rebbe's Army* in *Turning Judaism Outward*, Brooklyn: Kol Menachem, 2014, pages 337- 357).

From 1987 on the Rebbe encouraged his followers to open their eyes to discern the Divine hand in other current events. He envisioned the Messianic perfection of humanity as having political axis but that "we must do our part, and sometimes we will observe G-d doing His, but the goal is the same that *they may all call upon the name of G-d to serve Him with one consent*".

On the other hand, books abound that question the relevance of *organized religion* in this age of gene mapping, cybertechnology, nanotech etc. Do we still need to subscribe to an ancient and obsolete code of conduct as some would argue about Jewish morality, rituals and practices? Can we just raise children to be kind and respectful and choose which spirituality he will subscribe later when he becomes an adult? As Rabbi Yossy Goldman[36] articulated in his article at Chabad.org on Parshah "*Mishpatim*"; the "***ten commandments does not have an expiration date; notwithstanding all the medical and scientific discoveries, human nature itself has not changed and the moral issues our ancestors faced, are still challenging this current generation. Looking after aged parents is not a new problem, sibling rivalry, jealousy and warring nations are still headlines in our lifetime***".

As Rabbi Goldman continued "science and technology address the ***how and what of life***, but they do not answer the question of ***why*. Why are we here in the first place**?" These new innovations and scientific breakthroughs have unraveled many mysteries that puzzled us for centuries, but they have not answered a single moral question. Only the Torah addresses the moral minefield and those issues are more pressing today than ever before in history. Torah is truth, and truth is eternal. If we ever needed a Torah- we need it equally today and maybe more so as our moral compass to guide us daily. Children need structure and can be molded early in life; at Chabad, young and old are welcome and there is no age limit to learn Torah.

I'm reminded of a European couple who bemoaned to me that despite their material wealth, financially stable children, healthy grandchildren and in possession of all the trimmings of *success*; now that they are in their golden years, they're missing a sense of belongingness. They expressed that they're envious of Jews who have strong family and community connectivity and can literally connect with their tribe all over the world!

"Income inequality challenges economic cohesion as the classes divide. Demographic diversity challenges cultural cohesion as different ethnic groups rub against one another. The weakening of the social fabric has created a range of social problems, alienated young men to join *ISIS* or ISIL so they can have a sense of belonging. Racial animosity stubbornly exists, the liberation of the individual was supposed to lead to mass empowerment but it turns out that *people can effectively pursue their goals only when they know who they are – when they have firm identities.* Strong identities can come only when people are embedded in a rich social fabric.

We want to go off, create, explore and experiment with new ways of thinking and living; but we also want to be situated- embedded in loving families and enveloping communities, thriving within a healthy cultural infrastructure that provides us with values and goals". (David Brooks, *How Covenants Make Us*: New York Times, 2016)[37].

In shared Jewish life, we disagree in many occasions but we also love one another as evident when the world Jewry ached in unison for the acts of violence when three Jewish teenagers (Eyal Yifrach, Naftali Fraenkel and Gilad Shaar O.B.M.) were abducted and murdered in Israel in 2014. Each is a part of the Jewish nation; orthodox, conservative or unaffiliated Jews from Manila to Guatemala felt the pain of their parents and mourned the loss of these young Jewish lives. I prayed and ached with Jews all over the world, three lives too many for any family. There is a covenant that exists among Jews that maybe difficult to fathom for non- Jews; we understand that we're part of one another, a small, close-knit but significant tribe. It involves a vow to serve the relationship that is sealed by love as Ruth, the famous Jewish convert stated "Where you go, I will go, your people shall be my people".

I once coined the phrase to my husband "Chabad brings Jews back to Judaism" and I think in a nutshell that describes what the Chabad emissaries do. Chabad adherents were inspired to carry out the difficult work of painstakingly seeking out Jews who have become *lost* and deeply assimilated in the host culture. The Rebbe, Menachem Mendel Schneerson[35]O.B.M. an educator himself, noticed the youth's lack of obedience, not only of obedience to G-d, but also their general in-submission to authority including authority of parents at home and teachers in school and the authority of law and order in the streets. He believed that the cure was in attacking the cause and he came to a conclusion that there was no other way than trying to effect a basic change in the child's nature through a system of discipline and obedience to rules that he/she can be induced to get accustomed to. To be effective, he advocated that it be freely and readily accepted *without coercion*. Strict ***Sabbath observance*** and other ***mitzvot*** which have been the secrets of Jewish strength throughout the ages as the *secret weapon*. Having a personal relationship with God ingrained at an early age helps strengthen the foundation. (Chaim Miller, *Turning Judaism Outward* : Brooklyn: Kol Menachem, 2014, pages 339- 340).

Chabad embraced this position with vigor and currently the incredible growth that a grass roots- style autonomy has accomplished tremendous success, with more than 5200 emissaries all over the world gathered in New York during the ***Hakhel*** year in Nov. 2015. Young couples leave Brooklyn, New York almost weekly to carry out Chabad's work on distant shores. My personal experiences of so many Chabad emissaries from Florida to Manila and many cities is short of a miracle. In the past the presence of Coke used to be a barometer for civilization, nowadays in the Jewish world the presence of a Chabad shul is the new frame of reference. In 1996, when I first visited the **Ohel,** (Rebbe's grave) I was just beseeching for a Chabad house to open in Manila, now 20 years later there are four Chabad synagogues in the Philippines.

The Chabad house in Manila (Makati) successfully raised funds in a span of 24 hours the amount needed to build an 8 story synagogue thru Charidy.com and matched by equally magnanimous Jewish donors. This was a phenomenal outpouring of support in a day by Jews from all over the world and it is so uplifting to be part of this dynamic movement.

How do they do it? Is there any secret ingredient or is it a clandestine operation?

At my second visit to the World Lubavitch headquarters in October, 2015, I saw firsthand their dedication and serious learning ethics. They spend a year of ***shlichus,*** when the students would be sent as the Rebbe's emissaries to cities around the world. This is the time when we see them in our synagogue assisting the rabbis. This year is a time of personal growth for them, as young men find themselves in positions of responsibility. This is a brilliant and ingenuous way to train young minds and start showing their leadership skills while under the tutelage of the Chabad rabbis where they are assigned. It is a time of fun, exploration and contemplation since they are about to decide on their future. I've talked to a few of them and you can feel their enthusiasm and excitement of all the adventures and memorable experiences they had, one of them told me of his experience helping the Chabad rabbi in Asia and when he made a short trip to an island off Cebu, Philippines. Upon his arrival to this small islet and pension house where he stayed, the owner gave him a warm hug and was in tears and told him "all my life I've been praying that I meet a Jew and here G-d sent you to me". That's when he told me that Filipinos respect Jews a lot and refer to Israel as the "*Holy Land*" which may ring some truth since the Philippines has the 2nd lowest rate of antisemitism in the world ranked just higher than Myanmar[38].

The youth assisting the rabbis at Chabad have a wide range of personalities but their age belies their maturity and genuine enthusiasm in helping with the different activities at the synagogue. In Miami Beach, they offer Jewish tourists a chance to wrap *tefillin* or provide them with Shabbat candles for Friday night. They tell us stories of travelling to Chabad in Thailand or Nepal to help the rabbis during high holidays, and their excitement to be part of this "Roving Rabbis" program. These Chabad *yeshiva* students with their ubiquitous black hats, conservative suits and budding beards are familiar sights in major North American cities, in Europe and countries around the world. **Bochurim** (a young, unmarried Jewish man; a student in a Talmudic academy) - can be spotted carrying velvet bags with *tefillin* at the ready, just in case they find a Jew who has not donned the *tefillin* that day so they can offer him to perform that *mitzvah.*

Capturing the boundless energy and idealism of these youth and providing them the venue to learn by osmosis is parallel to an "internship" or as we call in the Philippine, OJT or on the job training. This process provides them a hands- on experience before becoming an emissary by observing, living and performing community outreach prior to becoming independent. I ponder if I had this type of experience, what impact would it have on me in my so called years of idealism? My cousin who worships at the Church of Latter Day Saints mentioned that they too have similar type of experience but only for men, with Chabad, women do this as well. The eldest daughter of Rabbi Yossi Harlig in Kendall area where we volunteer came back from Asia with an infectious enthusiasm of her exposure there, which will propel her to a life with purpose and trajectory and make a difference at such a young age.

CHAPTER 9

Learning Curves

Do you keep **kosher**? Is it hard? How do you go about it? These are questions I am frequently asked and I understand the curiosity and anxiety of someone who is contemplating of, or interested in going to the next level of keeping **kosher**.

Among the *kashrut* or *kosher* dietary laws are the prohibitions of the consumption of unclean animals such as pork and shellfish and most insects, mixture of meat and milk and the commandment to slaughter mammals and birds according to a process known as **shechita**. There are also laws regarding agriculture. It can be intimidating specially when no one is really coaching you one on one, or holding your hands as you go thru changes in your abode. Knowledge is power so I thought reading a book, attending lectures, keenly observing the kosher kitchens of the *rebbetzins*' home and observant congregants will be more than enough. Well, I found out that this is a gradual process as well that one has to incorporate into one's life. So, I didn't get discouraged despite the many errors I incurred along the way and made a conscious effort to make this a part of my life that I'm cognizant will take some time.

We started by not eating *Pork* since this is an ubiquitous presence in Asian dishes, avoiding shrimp and crabs was made easier by the fact that I'm allergic to Iodine.(I was given Epinephrine on a visit to Manila in 1983 after consuming this bottom dweller – shrimp ! Was I predestined?). I thought my methodical ways of gathering data and implementing them (as you know I'm a researcher too!) would suffice to prepare me but wrong….!!! . We purchased practice dishes and utensils, one set of cutlery had blue plastic handles for milk or **dairy** so we can get our brains to think and practice the habit of separating milk dishes and meat or **fleischig** (I dropped a spoon in the process of koshering our new cutlery when I immersed them in the ocean). Our kitchen was filled with blue labels for dairy, green for ***parve*** such as fish, vegetables and grains and red for meat. Mastery will take a sincere effort but over time it is becoming second nature to me.

I am not embarrassed to admit that nowadays, purchasing prepared food from Kosher establishments is a regular habit we do; paves for a more balanced life and gives me time to tend my coveted organic garden. I am able to pack tuna or chicken sandwiches for lunch and incorporate practical, healthy food choices with our weekly meal plans. When baking breads or cookies, I use coconut oil, almond or coconut milk; I refrain from using butter so I can make my dessert and eat it too even if we had meat as our main dish! I was determined to master the culinary challenge, my tennis coach used to tell me that he hit thousands of tennis balls before he perfected his serve; as the old adage goes *practice makes perfect.*

Trips back to the Philippines were daunting especially when we're invited to eat at friends' or relatives' homes. Once at a dinner, the Visayan version of a mouth- watering dish of young fern leaves or Fiddlehead fern (**pako,** sc. name: Athyrium Esculentum) on bottom dweller crabs, simmered in coconut milk with ginger was hard to resist. I politely picked the fern and ate them. (I know in the kosher world, this is forbidden since the crabs are ***treif*** (Yiddish word for non-kosher food) and pots and utensils did not undergo the koshering process). But my ***yetzar hara*** (evil inclination) tempted me or was it partly my attempt to appease my cousin whom we haven't seen for 20+ years? Maybe I reasoned out that I want to acknowledge my cousin's efforts to prepare a lavish dinner for our family. Him and his wife took time away from their busy medical practice to host this extravaganza, we had so much to talk about our lives that unfolded over the years.

We, Filipinos are very hospitable and whether we're rich or poor, lunch or dinner invitations are not rare occurrences when we go back home as a ***balikbayan*** (Filipino returning to the Philippines after having lived overseas for a period of time). On our first trip to my city of Baybay in the 1990's my friend's husband personally cracked the crabs for Robert when he noticed Robert's struggles in removing the meat of this scrumptious scavenger. The Pinoy's hospitality is world renowned and accepting invitations to break bread with loved ones was always a treat to me, now this offers me another opportunity to inform my host of my newfound spiritual direction and its dietary restrictions. I am careful not to overindulge the time given to explain myself, I never impose on my hosts, if asked what I eat, I would just tell them I don't eat any pork and shellfish. I use my intuition and sensitivity to the hosts when discussing this matter. My immediate family refrains from preparing any pork dishes and warns me. Most of the time, I still have to be the vigilant one because they may use *Hebi* or young dried shrimp on the ***pancit*** or noodle dish commonly served on birthdays and special occasions; I always bring different nuts with me as well . Remember, NOT to judge unless you are in the same shoes. Now I can comprehend the different personal challenges and cultural processes one goes thru to observe *kosher* laws. Just imagine the sacrifices the Chabad **schluchim** (emissary) went thru when they opened synagogues in different corners of the world, be it Nepal, or Cambodia, hats off to them for their conviction and commitment to the Torah laws of **kashrut**.

For those sushi lovers like me, it was particularly challenging to stop my craving for the roe of the sea urchins (**uni**). Honestly, it took me a long while to bid my last farewell to these spiny, pricey little munchies. On our first family reunion, we visited "Cuatro Islas" or four small islands, with pinkish to white sand beaches about a half hour boat ride from our city where we paid a mere $1.00 for a pail full of these echinoderms. The fee included the labor of teenage boys who dove to catch and split them right in-front of us. In Asia, sea urchins are considered aphrodisiacs and must have caused my much delayed awakening that my *uni* delicacies are bottom dwellers, feeding primarily on algae and are *treif.* Later, a Filipino sushi chef my husband and I met at a *kosher* sushi bistro in Miami Beach would entice us with his coconut flaked crab imitation sushi rolls and other *kosher* Japanese food substitutions. I must admit, the taste is not the same but over time, I learned to control my impulses. Even the fried soft shell crab that used to be our favorite food is now just a blur in our memories!

Despite the many classes I have attended, there's always more to learn and incorporate regarding *kosher* observance. Once, I sponsored a women's breakfast and I was so excited to bring organic, Kosher milk with the symbol (OU) clearly on the label but much to my chagrin, I brought the wrong milk! What...? I thought and learned that milk in the USA is considered kosher and the kosher symbol is clearly written ! Lo and behold, I realized later on that the milk required for this gathering has to be **Cholov Israel ! (**Milking and bottling is done under the supervision of a *Mashgiach* and milk is only coming from *kosher* animal). I felt dejected, all the organic milk I bought I brought back home and the rabbi had to get *Cholov Israel* milk from his house to serve the guests! Some observant people may not be aware as well that there are now many *kosher* certifications and to get updates I bought a magazine that I had purchased in a kosher store that showed the different symbols for certification and updates of the products such as KM-Kosher Miami, OU- Union of Orthodox, KSA etc.

Parsha **Shemini**[39] introduces the Torah's dietary laws. Animals must chew their cud and have split hooves to be kosher, fish need fins and scales and there's a list of forbidden fowl. Kosher is not for physical health but for **spiritual health**. The *kosher* rule is considered a **chukah.** *Chukkim (plural for Chukah)* are those mitzvot, such as the dietary laws *(kosher*) or the laws of family purity, which Jews accept as divine decrees, despite their incomprehensibility and -- in the most extreme of *chukkim* -- their irrationality. One develops better control of impulses and increases patience; I think before I act, say or even buy something; could it be due to the pause you have to do and being conscious of what you put in your mouth as well as **the half to one hour waiting period before eating meat after consuming a dairy meal? However, one has to wait 6 hours after consuming meat (fleischig) food**

before one can eat dairy food! This is a good practice for mindfulness; a guest who came to our Sukkot party years ago gave me this tip; I was wandering why she ate the dairy ice cream first then mingled with everyone before she ate the *fleischig* or meat main dishes !

Oftentimes, what really defines a *Jewish Home* – is the kitchen, it extends a warm and eloquent invitation to all fellow Jews that *you are welcome here.* Children may also be trained to delay gratification in the purchase of the latest toy, technology or I-phone; patience and discipline is subtly incorporated thru the *kosher mitzvah.* I also get fascinated when people would ask **"is that kosher to do or act"**? It seems that the secular world also gauges the authenticity or legality of an object or an action and if confirmed, then it is alluded to as **acceptable** and **"kosher"**.

On the wedding ceremony of Robert's cousin, the reception was held at our condominium. The couple did not have the **right kosher** wine and this time (you guessed it right) we took pride in taking out our supply from home. We had **Mevushal kosher** wines that we gladly served the guests and the rabbi was so glad we had them in stock. Now, it's getting a little technical but below is just a little information how to distinguish the two types of wines.

Kosher wines- for it to be considered, must contain only kosher ingredients. According to traditional Jewish law, once the grapes are picked and brought to be crushed, only Shabbat-observant Jews can be involved in making the wine. From crushing to bottling, kosher wine must be handled exclusively by observant Jews. **Mevushal** (literally "cooked") wine has been heated to the point that idol worshippers wouldn't use it for their nefarious purposes. It turns out even idol worshippers had standards for their wine. They wouldn't use wine for an offering if it had been boiled because boiling wine removes much of the flavor. So the rabbis ruled that in order to avoid the possibility of a Jew ever drinking wine that was idolatry-associated, only cooked wine could be served to a Jew by a non-Jew). *Mevushal* wines are usually used by the orthodox community and the rabbi specifically ordered this kind of wine for consumption at this wedding.

My cousin who is a member of the Church of Latter Day Saints sent me a link of Prof. Walter Veith's[40] You Tube(TR)video about "The Science Behind Biblical Clean and Unclean Foods". This non –Jewish professor explained that there are scientific reasons for clean and unclean animals and are generally divided into carnivores and scavengers. Cows and sheep are kosher and they eat plant food; have cloven hooves and chew their cud (they regurgitate), have a rumen or pre-stomach in which bacteria ferment and has the least accumulation of toxins. Camel is **not** kosher; is adapted to desert environment; conserves water, doesn't sweat and retains urea that is dissipated to the flesh of the animal and has less excretion and higher toxic load; likewise, horse doesn't have split hooves and a rumen and is not kosher! Fish with fins and scales are kosher and do not retain as much salt as sharks which are not. **Pig is unclean**, eats anything, is a scavenger, with high level of toxins, carries a lot of microorganisms and has capacity to harbor viruses and pathogenic organisms. He further detailed the scientific rationale to explain biblical or Judaism's *kosher* dietary rules. An elated phone call from my sister who declared that when she was strolling the beach of her ocean front house she observed the shrimps and crabs eating dirt, hence she declared " why should we eat seafood that thrive on eating dirt?". We are what we eat, that was an AHA moment for her!

"The food that we eat becomes a part of us, sustaining us and giving us energy to serve God. *Kosher* food has a positive and spiritually sensitizing influence on the soul, bringing you closer to God." (Chaim Miller, Torah- The Five Books of Moses. New York, Lifestyle Books, 2011, p.638).

CHAPTER 10

Queen Esther And The Purim Feast

MY FIRST PURIM HOLIDAY, SEEMED like Halloween but I was skeptical because we had to attend services in the synagogue. The costumes of the children dazzled me when families came for the services. Halloween is not a Jewish holiday but thank G-d we have *Purim which* is very festive and fun. It celebrates the deliverance of the Jews from their enemies in the biblical *Book of Esther*. Kids love this holiday and rabbis and their families along with congregants are decked with different creative attires or you can come in any dress as you please except no nudists aloud. This year we took wacky, crazy pictures with weird pauses with our JAP (Jewish American Pinay) friends since this occasion gives as an excuse to be who we really are "eccentric".

Purim is so-called because the villain of the story, Haman, cast the **"pur"** (the lot) against the Jews yet failed to destroy them. The younger generation may consider having a masquerade ball similar to a Halloween party in the Christian world. I've witnessed Japanese, Mexican or sports themed parties. In college campuses this holiday is a big fund raiser and an event to look forward to because for some un-affiliated Jewish college students the revelry experienced during Purim at Chabad may be a catalyst for students to start attending Shabbat dinners. It is a lot of fun but at the same time Purim is a reminder of this constant threat that the Jewish people encounter.

The heroes are "*Esther*, a beautiful young Jewish woman living in Persia (now, Iran, déjà vu ?) and her cousin Mordecai, who raised her as if she were his daughter. Esther was taken to the house of Ahasuerus, king of Persia, to become part of his harem. King Ahasuerus loved Esther more than his other women and made Esther queen, but the king did not know that Esther was a Jew, because Mordecai told her not to reveal her identity. The villain of the story is Haman, an arrogant, egotistical advisor to the king. Haman hated Mordecai because Mordecai refused to bow down to Haman, so Haman plotted to destroy the Jewish people.

Many have noted the echoes of Purim in the Nuremberg war crime trials. In the Book of Esther, Haman's ten sons were hanged (Esther 9:13); in 1946, ten of Hitler's top associates were put to death by hanging for their war crimes (including the crime of murdering 6 million Jews). An 11th associate of Hitler; Hermann Goring, committed suicide the night before the execution, a parallel to the suicide of Haman's daughter recorded in the Talmud[41] (Rebecca Benhamou, Times of Israel, Dec. 2012).

One of the more meaningful gestures I enjoy during Purim is sending **mishloach mano**t (baskets filled with food and drink) to other Jews. According to Jewish law each *mishloach manot* must contain at least two different kinds of food that is ready to eat. Most synagogues coordinate these activities in their congregation. Some women volunteer to prepare these baskets of gifts and this is another form of getting together for worthy causes. As usual, festive meals, called the Purim se'udah (meal) is a big part of this holiday celebration. We love eating **hamantaschen** which are special Purim cookies, during the dessert course.

In addition to sending *mishloach manot*, Jews are also commanded to be especially charitable during Purim. Jews will often make monetary donations to charities they support during this time or will give money to needy people.

An interesting yet well-received commandment related to Purim has to do with drinking. According to Jewish law, adults of drinking age are supposed to get so drunk that they can't tell the difference between Mordechai (a hero in the Purim story) and Haman (the villain). At our synagogue, Vodka and other forms of liquor will overflow and sometimes the situation can really get out of hand. Not everyone participates in this custom and recovering alcoholics and people with health problems are exempt altogether. This drinking tradition stems from the joyous nature of Purim. (Of course, it goes without saying that if you choose to participate in this custom you should drink responsibly by arranging for a safe ride after your celebrations).

CHAPTER 11

Mikvahs, Mitzvahs And Mezuzahs (Who Doesn't Like M & M's?)

I KNOW, I KNOW, IT's getting complicated, the only similarities are the phonetics. The primary meaning of the *Hebrew* word ***mitzvah*** is commandment. It refers to any of the collection of the 613 commandments or precepts in the Torah that relate chiefly to the religious and oral conduct of Jews. It also refers to any good or praiseworthy deed.

One of the laws of Family Purity (***Taharat HaMishpacha***) that governs marital intimacy is that when a woman begins her menstrual cycle, she and her husband don't touch each other for around two weeks (the time of her flow plus one additional week). After a woman immerses in a **mikvah** (ritual bath), they reunite, until her cycle begins again.

For almost two weeks out of the month, a woman is off-limits to her husband for physical affection and intimacy, which builds up excitement for their reunion. (I'm reminded of our Hispanic speaking patients telling their children when they're in the eye exam room "mira pero no toca" which means, you can look but you can't touch. But even being apart can be good for the relationship. The cycle of *Taharat HaMishpachah* keeps a couple's intimate life on their radar at all times.

It's no coincidence that a menstrual cycle is usually 28-30 days long, coinciding with the cycle of the moon. Just like the moon waxes and wanes, the uterine lining sheds blood and then replenishes again. Apparently, G-d feels that a marriage needs a monthly dose of fresh air and rejuvenation. It's not only the separation that can make a relationship fresh, but the immersion in the *mikvah.*

Mikvah immersion is one of the most controversial comments among our Jewish friends, some of them would say this mitzvah is so "old fashioned" yet when they hear the rationale they give me incredulous stares yet the response unanimously is "wow, that's amazing, I didn't know that". The period of monthly abstention actually leads to a monthly renewal of marriage. The custom of modesty is more accepted and easier to understand such as wearing long skirts and no sleeveless dresses but *mikvah* draws a lot of opposing views among Jews in the secular world.

As Rohel Holzkenner[42] beautifully wrote "if you look through a G-dly lens, you can see the absolute beauty and divine brilliance of the human menstrual cycle- it hardwires a marriage with a natural system of separation and reunion. Women do not need to guess at when to pull back, we just need to listen to our body. In a relationship with another, passion makes us run closer to the other person, while returning creates boundaries. Together, run and return create balance. Inherent within a woman's body is the guided choreography of a G-d centered marriage."

One gets immersed and is mesmerized by the beauty and significance of age old traditions handed down from generation to generation. It is no surprise that my association and Jewish conversion has opened up a different world for me.

The *mitzvah* of putting the **mezuzah** now has more meaning and personal connection after a series of life changing experiences. We thought our previous house had the properly installed mezuzah until we learned that it did not have the *kosher* parchment that contains the prayer that is supposed to be placed inside the shell. Throughout all those years technically Robert and his parents only had the front door **mezuzah decor**! (this truth is revealed with Robert's permission!). We learned by default after we moved to Miami Beach so we can be "*Shomer Shabbos*", when the rabbi placed the mezuzah with the *kosher* parchment inside each of them and placed strategically on all the doors except the bathrooms. Secondly, we're supposed to check these mezuzahs every couple of years preferably before *Rosh Hoshana* (Jewish New Year) to make sure they're kosher (ie. parchment has intact *Hebrew* letters).

Our compelling **mezuzah** story continues to unfold with my husband's office move in January of 2007. We dreaded packing boxes, charts, thousands of eyeglass frames and contact lenses, but had no choice since the new owner of the building had other plans. After requesting Rabbi Zev Katz to kindly put the mezuzah **after** our move, his father, Rabbi Fishel Katz, interfered firmly yet assertively and with his booming voice stated "You **should put the mezuzah first before you move anything for an** *EEEEAAAASSSSYYYYY MOOOOVE!*" We didn't think twice about his advice and to our delight, my 2 brothers and a very organized and extremely meticulous sister in law flew in from California to help and the super in demand ophthalmic technician "just happens to have 2 days before he leaves for his family winter vacation" to set up the ophthalmic equipment and optical area . To top it all, the building owner had excess cabinets from another unit that he gladly donated to us with a market value of $20,000 -$25,000. We had a blast with this move, bonded with family on our frequent Home Depot (TR) trips, our staff felt relieved that the burden was not strictly on their shoulders. Now, who says a move is fun, it is considered one of the most stressful times in one's life but we all admit we didn't get stressed, in fact we had so much fun that my brothers ask " when is Robert moving again so we can be there ?". Now, I'm divulging them the secret of that EASY MOVE !

Since the move, we've had patients who admitted that they found Dr. Grand's name in the insurance book but chose Robert because of his name and because of this (pointing to the *mezuzah*). In retrospect we also understand a homeowner's response when we were searching for a house in Miami Beach, we asked him "do you have a house alarm system?". He shook his head with an emphatic *NO*, kissed the *mezuzah* and confidently said "this is my security".

CHAPTER 12

Tribal Holidays

THE KOSHER KING OF MIAMI and our favorite bakery *Zak the Baker*(TR) in the Wynwood area of Miami gets due credit since I first found these words on his website during Passover to warn his customers of their closure for the holidays. Tribal holiday resonates better that all the long explanations of the Jewish Holidays since there are many and depending on your level of observance it can be overwhelming and confusing initially.

There are **Three Pilgrimage Festivals** namely: **Pesach (Passover**), **Shavuot (Weeks**) and **Sukkot (Tents or Booths**) when the Israelites living in the Kingdom of Judah would make a pilgrimage to Temple in Jerusalem, as commanded by the Torah. In my morning prayers, the pilgrimage offering when appearing before the Lord on the three festivals are mentioned in the *Book of Deuteronomy* and *Book of Exodus*: "Offer a sacrifice to Me three times each year. Keep the festival of **Matzos** [i.e., unleavened bread] ... the reaping festival [i.e., **Shavuot]** ... the harvest festival [i.e., **Sukkot**]. ... Three times each year, every male among you must appear before God the Lord ..." (Exodus 23:14–17) ...When you bring in the products of your threshing floor and wine vat, you shall celebrate the festival of **Sukkot** for seven days.

Pesach-. The term means *to pass over* and commemorates the release of the Jewish people from bondage in the land of Egypt. *Pesach* is observed for eight days, (seven in Israel). This is literally 'the festival of *matzot* (unleavened bread). During this period, it is a commandment to eat *matzah* as the Torah states "Seven days you shall eat unleavened bread" (Exodus 12:15). (Due to their rush to get out, the Jews had a few minutes to prepare, I would be too, *Pharaoh* might change his mind !).

The challenge on this holiday is the spring cleaning to ensure no ***chometz*** or unleavened bread, crumbs or crackers are lurking in the house. There's also an internal challenge as well; our determination to make sure not to eat leavened bread. One of the lessons inculcated on this holiday is the importance of humility; no air remember ? Our bowels will complain because bathroom breaks may take longer than usual since **matzot** are compact and dense so to counteract this dilemma, we make sure we consume ample amount of fruits, water and green vegetables (juicing with pears, spinach, carrots and celery is perfect for this time, spring cleaning of the colon). We never miss our walking exercises to hasten our gastric motility during this unleavened flat bread festival.

Passover, the story of G-ds miracle of the splitting of the sea and the ten plagues that forced Pharaoh to free the Israelites usually coincides with the "*Holy Week*" in the Christian world hence a picture that is commonly seen in a Filipino home is the "Last Supper" with Jesus and the twelve apostles; we had a wooden carving of this depiction by the *Igorots* (native people of Baguio, Phil.) hanging in our dining room. Most Christians are not aware that the *Last Supper* was the Jewish holiday of **Passover**, even my close friends and family couldn't believe it, so I just tell them to google it.

One of the most indelible experiences we had of Passover was at Chabad of Cebu, Philippines in April, 2014. During our arrival at the shul, there were only more than a dozen people, so the rabbi who just flew in from Israel about a week prior to the holiday as a substitute rabbi, was just getting to know the area. We took pictures outside to document this holiday, then the rabbi asked our opinion if he should just fold the many tables and chairs he set –up since it was almost candle lighting time and less than 20 showed up. He was concerned that there will be no *minyan*. We advised him not to, thankfully we were credible to him, because just after nightfall, approximately 85 Israeli backpackers showed up and overwhelmed the air-conditioner. We had to hold our call for nature because it was not easy to leave our seats. He could hardly finish the drinking of the 4 cups because the place got so noisy and chaotic in a vibrant and joyful way. Singing of Jewish melodies prevailed and the conversation was now difficult to control. That's a Jewish experience that I'm getting used to and crave, together as one family, young adults spend months backpacking in Thailand, New Zealand or the Philippines after their military stint in Israel. Most are non-observant Jews but when it comes to Pesach, their souls miss home and they usually find the comforts of a far flung Chabad shul. Last April, 2016 Chabad Cebu hosted about 300 guests for this holiday.

Chabad.org has a wealth of information, after Passover, it's a great time to review the You Tube(TR) video classes of Chana Rachel Schusterman, "The Kabbalah of Self- Refinement" which is our task during this period when we count the Omer for 49 days (7 weeks) until the giving of the Torah[43]. According to Ms. Schusterman, "this is a time of preparation and self- refinement of our emotional character traits and thereby transform ourselves and be able to receive the Torah". The first week is a time of ***chesed***, our ability to love and who we are meant to be hence this is the first. We emulate G-ds kindness to us, we want to see the good in others; we work on **giving** in the right and positive way. Each trait works with the other traits and help us actualize our purpose; when refined; it balances with the other traits. It is exemplified by biblical personalities such as ***chesed*** by Abraham who provided physical and spiritual sustenance to his guests and emulated G-d's loving kindness. Each week and each day, when the Jews travelled in the desert they focused on loving G-d. We can care about other persons by giving them the benefit of the doubt, care in unselfish way and the seven weeks allow us to polish our character so we can actualize a higher purpose. **Chesed** is followed by **gevurah** (strength).

Each day and each week another facet of our emotions are balanced and refined. There are ten *Sefirots*, the ten qualities or attributes through which G-d manifests himself; **chochmah**-wisdom, **binah**-understanding, **daat**-knowledge, **chesed**-kindness, **gevurah**-strength, **tiferet**-beauty, **netzach**-victory, **hod**-splendor, **yesod**- foundation and **malchut**- kingship. Hmm, I'm peeking your interest but this concept to me is so deep and requires the proper guidance of a rabbi with *Kabbalah* expertise; it is one of the most fascinating aspects of Judaism, (popularized by some Hollywood celebrities); I still have a lot to learn. I've attended classes on this topic at the Jewish learning institute lecture series but I'm still at the very early phase of learning ***kabbalah*** (the soul of Judaism). Weekly lectures are offered at different Chabad houses. Occasionally, I do admit, several times I forget to count the Omer but I don't beat myself, I try my very best to learn and study as I become more immersed in my observance of Judaism.

Taking days off when you have a small business definitely tested our trust in the Almighty and in the words of an acquaintance, one technically needs a month off during this period. Advanced financial planning is essential as well but the most important is believing that *Hashem* will take care of the rest. We can attest to small miracles and G-d's hands when we first started observing taking days off on the 2nd day of these **Yom Tov** (high holidays). Once, we succumbed to the temptation of working on the 2nd day of ***Rosh Hoshana*** to accommodate a family who were Orthokeratology patients of my husband (with humility, I'll divulge that my husband as of this writing is the only Fellow of the International Academy of Orthokeratology[44] in Miami- Dade county with expertise in the tedious process of molding corneas to correct nearsightedness) and the family chose that day for their appointments since one of the children was an out- of town college student. Expecting a great income that day, we were dismayed when the mother called an hour after their scheduled appointment that they had a car trouble and the family couldn't come in, so you can just imagine how that affected our bottom line!

We were not stubborn to repeat the same mistake so the following year, we made sure NOT to work on the 2nd days of **Yom tov** and NOT to my surprise, a few days prior to the holidays, we signed in 2 Orthokeratology patients from out of town. The fees covered our office expenses for the holidays. Skeptics can deduce their own conclusions but G-d was watching for sure. Similar blessings have been repeated to us in different Jewish holidays so you know we don't worry that G-d provides for our **parnasah** or means of living but we do our part of the bargain.

Shavuot- is the festival of the giving of the Torah (Ten commandments). The second of the three Pilgrim Festivals is celebrated for 2 days outside Israel (and in Israel for 1 day). The name **shavuot** means "*weeks*" because it occurs 7 weeks after the 2nd day of Pesach. It falls on the 6th day of Sivan (approximately May/June). All night studying at the shul is a typical activity the night before this holiday to make sure we're not asleep when the Ten commandments were given as in the days of old to ensure we don't miss this momentous occasion. Lots of caffeine are served at this time with cookies!

We spent one Shavuot in Jerusalem and the experience was magical. As customary when visiting these ancient walls, we placed our written prayers in between the cracks and you may have seen this repeated by presidents or heads of state when they visit Israel. (I'm sure they don't want to miss this opportunity, just imagine the weight on their shoulders, being the head of their countries, they need all the help, be they Jews or non- Jews!). While I was there, I felt like I was nearer to G-d than anywhere else I have prayed, this is just a personal experience so try it yourself when you visit Jerusalem!

All the fresh fruits and vegetables in season were prominently displayed everywhere and were delectable and you can feel the air of renewal in the atmosphere. During Shavuot, dishes made of dairy such as cheeses are in abundance and blintzes and ice cream are often served in many synagogues.

Originally a harvest festival, **Sukkot** was given added historical significance as a commemoration of the exodus from Egypt, when the Jewish people had to live in temporary dwellings whilst they lived in the desert before entering the *Promised Land.* Observant Jews will eat all their meals including breakfast under the **Sukka**. This is actually my personal favorite holiday because it is a transformational experience to me eating under a **Sukka** and I like imagining G-d's protective clouds when Jews were wandering in the desert, Florida is cooler by a degree or two and the air gets crisper and humidity is lower !

A **"Sukka"** or temporary dwelling is generally made of palm fronds but with the visibility of stars at night, it gives us a chance to really appreciate the significance of gratitude; savor what we have, after-all, everything in life is fleeting or temporary, Hashem or G-d is in charge and we can submit our concerns to Him . During the 40 years in the desert, G-d protected the Jews with clouds of glory and this is apropos today and in the future. My brothers once helped build a **Sukka** for us, they followed the instructions in my book as I tried to explain to them the best I can the reason for this dwelling. We also had a memorable "*wet and rainy Sukkot*" at Chabad in Kendall in 1995 when it started pouring while we were having dinner under the Sukkah and the baked chicken became chicken soup.

The Four Species- The year 2015 marked the first year that we purchased ***lulav*** and ***etrog*** . We were picking up a book from Aspaclaria(TR) Judaica store in North Miami when shipment of the "*four species*" arrived from Morocco (due to the **Schmitta** year – Sabbath or 7th year of the agricultural cycle in Israel). We got compelled to do one more mitzvah after being in awe of the different types of species and how the store staff and customers were meticulously inspecting and handling them like they were diamonds! The store assistant gently coached my husband on how to perform the mitzvah and we got hooked. (Who really wants to pay close to $100.00 for this package that include an elongated greenish yellow fruit, branches and palm fronds?). As you know it is quite intimidating, honestly we had sincere desire to purchase the set in the past, but if the amiable store manager Mendel wasn't there to encourage us and guide Robert of the details, we probably would have postponed this mitzvah again for the following year because we get intimidated for lack of knowledge on what to do!

We delayed our cantor's role in performing his job on the eve of Sukkot services because unbeknownst to us the **Lulav** knot has to be tied before *Yom tov* (sundown prior to the Sukkot Holiday, I told you we still have a lot to learn by osmosis), thankfully he was patient with us.

The concept of unity is so central to this mitzvah that it is reflected not only in the requirement of taking all four species together but also in the characteristics of the individual components of the mitzvah. The four species were intended to symbolize the final harvest and the fertility of the land. **Etrog** is one of the four kinds of plants known in Hebrew as the ***Arbah Minim*** (four species). The **Hadasi** (myrtle twigs) have a good smell but no taste, symbolizes the doer, the person with a lot of *mitzvot* but no serious learning. The **Lulav** (palm branch) has great taste but no smell. This symbolizes the committed scholar, a person with vast knowledge yet has little sweat equity in *mitzvot*. The **Aravot** (willow branches) have neither taste nor smell, symbolizes the nondescript, the person who lives the plainest life.

The **Etrog** (**Esrog** or Citron) tastes and smells wonderful; symbolizes the achiever- the person whose great Torah scholarship is matched by high *mitzvah* activity; hence observant Jews will pay big bucks to purchase the best *esrog* they can afford. The motif of unity is also reflected in the *esrog* because it represents a category of people whose potential for achievement is greater than that of others, its emphasis on unity must be greater. We must learn from the *esrog*, and not merely tolerate people of all kinds, including those with characters and personalities different from our own, but actually grow through contact with their divergent perspectives. Could this be the reason also why Jews will try to choose the most perfect *Etrog*, no blemish and some will pay any price to get the best? hmmm.

Don't be surprised if you see Jews ritually shaking these species under the **sukka** during this Holiday. A colleague at Jackson Memorial Hospital in Miami gave me a curious look (she thought I was going nuts!) when she saw me shaking the *Lulav* and *Etrog* to 6 different directions (north, south, east, west, up and down) inside a "hut" with the guidance of a rabbi (women are allowed to do this mitzvah), so I casually explained to her afterwards, she didn't realize I had converted to Judaism already.

In Miami Beach, you will find observant homes with their **sukka** pitched outside their homes that look like tents and meals are shared with friends and family under this structure. My women's Thursday Torah class also had our Torah and Tea held under the **sukka** during this week and some of the women who had their first experience of Sukkot were so excited that half of them were taking pictures of the whole class under the temporary dwelling.

One of the most beautiful sights to watch, (pictures are not allowed on *Yomtov* or Jewish holidays), is the circling by men around the ***bimah*** (sanctuary) seven times carrying their *lulav* and *esrog* during the **hakafot** *(going around).* Fathers and sons walking together with all other men and their sons, as one unit holding carefully their *Arbah Minim.* This profound closeness of sharing an important ritual with their fathers is a bond that boys can cherish as they grow up; fosters a closer relationship among men and their sons in the congregation. Last year, I witnessed a father from Argentina with his 3 sons during *Hakafot* and the emotions captured at this marvelous gathering was indeed a sight to behold, sublime; hence, it is etched forever in my mind.

Sometimes, I forget that although I am a convert, because I have been attending a Chabad- orthodox synagogue for 20 + years, to some Jews these holidays could actually still be a discovery to them. On occasion, I actually get inquiries from Jewish friends on the different meanings of the holidays and I am very humbled and grateful that I embraced Judaism and learned living to be a Jew gradually because the Torah is more alive and meaningful to me.

CHAPTER 13

Repentance, Prayer And Charity

DO WE NEED ALL OF the above, can we just be kind, compassionate and love one another? I would like to paraphrase Rabbi Jonathan Sacks[45] who gave an in-depth explanation that differs from the more commonly held notion of the meaning of *Teshuvah, Tefilla and Tzedakah.* These words we hear repeatedly on the months of ***Elul*** (around September/October in the Gregorian calendar) during the Jewish Holidays.

"During the ten days of **teshuvah**, we have the opportunity through our service, to cause G-d to grant us yet greater benefits from *His full and expansive hand* . *Teshuvah* means *returning* to the old, to one's original nature, underlying that concept is the fact that the Jew is, in essence, good. Desires or temptations may deflect him temporarily from being himself, being true to his essence but the bad that he does is not part of, nor does it affect, his real nature. Hence, *teshuvah* is a return to the self. **Tefillah** means *prayer.* It is our conversation with God. A person seeks to attach himself to G-d. It is man reaching towards G-d and is appropriate to everyone and at every time. The Jewish soul has a bond with G-d; but it also inhabits a body, whose preoccupation with the material world may attenuate that bond. It has to constantly be strengthened and renewed hence it is the function of *tefillah*. **Tzedakah** means *righteousness or justice*. The donor gives because it is his duty. Firstly, everything in the world belongs ultimately to G-d. A man's possessions are not his by right, rather, they are entrusted to him by G-d, and one of the conditions of that trust is that he should give to those who are *in need*. Secondly, man has a duty to act towards others as he asks G-d to act towards him". G-d for His blessings though He owes us nothing and is under no obligation. So we are bound in justice to give to those who ask us, even though we are in no way in their debt. In this way we are rewarded: measure for measure. Because we give freely, G-d gives freely to us. These are the three paths which lead to a year "*written and sealed*" for good. **By returning to one's innermost self *(teshuvah)*, by attaching oneself to G-d *(tefillah)* and by distributing one's possessions with righteousness *(tzedakah)*,** one turns the promise of Rosh Hashanah into the abundant fulfillment of **Yom Kippur**: A year of *sweetness and plenty*. (Rabbi Jonathan Sacks, *Teshuvah, Tefilla and Tzedakah* : Chabad.org).

I personally had to postpone the start of my new career opportunities to accommodate these holidays since they occur a few days from each other; if you are not independently employed, it can pause a challenge to your work schedule. In retrospect, the observance of these holidays prompted me to pursue careers that valued my talent and respected my holy days. I find that I get the "high" of the holidays before I go back to the reality of making a living. Most people if they are not granted vacation days will choose to take off on ***Yom Kippur.***

ROSH HASHANA- The Jewish New Year and **Yom Kippur** are the 2 most important holidays that non-observant Jews will observe. When I first started celebrating them with my husband, like most Jews, we would have dinner with family or friends on the eve of *Rosh Hashana*, then go to service on the first day of *Rosh Hoshana* and join friends and family again for the second night. We always had a marvelous time catching up with everyone. Honestly, it was more of a family gathering/ festive holiday dinner. Nowadays this holiday has evolved into a time of deep and profound self- introspection. The Chabad synagogues in Miami Beach has an open door policy, hence, together with our *Bagel and Pancit* club friends, we spend this holiday together along with consuming the festive meals initiated with a dip of apple on honey symbolically asking G-d for a "sweet" New Year!

Rosh Hashana is the anniversary of the creation of Adam and Eve, which highlights the special relationship between G-d and humanity. We express this deep connection by recognizing G-d as the literal and constant *Master of the Universe* and ourselves as his cherished creations. We also adopt a positive attitude for the year ahead, confident that G-d wants the best for us and will grant us the power needed to succeed as His agents.

Thankfully, the synagogues usually offer classes to provide an in-depth review of the significance, relevance or references found in the Torah of the many different holidays. The rabbi's wife incorporate many other practical tips such as how to set up a festive table or arrange cooking classes on recipes appropriate for the holiday. It is always a great learning experience although I have attended so many of these women's classes, I find something new to try in observance of the holiday celebration such as more dazzling and creative centerpieces using fruits or new dishes for *Rosh*

Hoshana. My deeper understanding of the true meaning of these holidays are enhanced and these immersive classes are transformational in how we conduct our lives.

The **tashlich**[46] (to cast) prayer ceremony recited next to a body of water performed on the first day of *Rosh Hoshana* is particularly significant . We shake our clothes, a tangible act to achieve the spiritual goal of shaking our sins from our soul. Jewish mysticism teaches that water corresponds to the attribute of kindness; in Miami Beach, we usually perform this near the Miami Beach Convention Center and the Botanical Garden.

A pomegranate is also eaten symbolizing our wish to have a year full of *mitzvot* and good deeds as a pomegranate is filled with luscious seeds. There are other symbolic foods eaten such as head of a fish (head of the class), carrots (meren in Yiddish means to multiply). Then, ten days of **teshuva** (repentance) starts on this holiday and ends on **Yom Kippur**.

During **Yom Kippur** (day of atonement), we stay in the synagogue for intense prayers of repentance and asking G-d for forgiveness. Fasting has always been a challenge for me. I observe my husband's determination and how disciplined and committed he is, that he can last 25 hours with no food nor water and doesn't even wet his lips at all. Since then I have gradually learned and have had easier fasts, usually at 4 pm I would have to drink orange juice because I get dizzy with splitting headaches. Just imagine walking for more than a mile back and forth to shul with no water in the Miami heat, however, 3 years ago, we started staying at a nearby hotel to spend the holidays. After more practice, sheer determination and Hashem's help, my fasts have been smoother. People with medical conditions are exempt to fast but it is best to ask the rabbi's opinion on this matter so you won't go astray.

A hundred sounds are blown from a ram's horn, the **shofar** during this solemn day and at the end of the service . Its call strikes the innermost chords of the soul as we coronate G-d as King of the Universe. **Yom Kippur** is capped with a light breaking of the fast by sundown and at the end of the service this is when everyone will wish each other "*next year in Jerusalem*" (the city of peace- a place of peace between body and soul, heaven and earth, the ideal and reality; when our body becomes a vehicle for the soul's expression, when the world values goodness and generosity over selfish gain; when we are at peace with ourselves and the world). *Jerusalem* is an ideal that Jews struggle to reach since it is a long journey from "Egypt" which symbolize two opposite spiritual states. Breaking the fast (not breakfast) is the term used that refers to the simple, festive light meals that synagogues usually provide after the services and these usually comprise of orange juice, bagels, lox, fruits and cakes which are easy to digest after a 25 hour fast.

It is customary to give **tzedakah** or charity during the weekdays of these 10 days for charity is a great source of merit and serves as protection against harsh decrees. You will notice that in most Chabad synagogues, they do not charge membership fees and congregants voluntarily give donations which I think is strategic in the financial success of the organization because from our 20 + years of experience when one is not coerced to give to charity but is just encouraged and gently reminded, a person will give freely and most of the time the amount given exceeds a membership fee. We personally like to donate books, sponsor a lecture for out of town speakers, or cater lunch or a meal but as in any charitable endeavors, the choice is ours.

Chabad is sensitive about the complaints of some congregants in other traditional synagogues of requiring tickets to attend the high holidays hence they are pragmatic and maintain an open door policy. Most synagogues will have envelopes that you can mail your donations or one can just log in to their websites for the much appreciated *Tzedakah* so they can maintain the different programs and community services they provide. Most Chabad synagogues rely on the generosity of congregants or charge nominal fees for Shabbat dinners and major holiday celebrations.

Judaism teaches us the importance of gratitude and to care for one another; people send donations or ***tzedakah*** to thank G-d for their blessings, to honor special occasions be it a Bar or Bat Mitzvah, birthday or wedding anniversary or in memory of dearly departed loved ones. The High Holidays is the only time in most Chabad houses that you will notice the Rabbi offering congregants the privilege to be honored to be called up to give **aliyah** or the rabbi will auction to the bidders or those who want to buy the *Aliyah.* It took me some time to get used to this bidding process but nowadays, I actively participate in this privilege to offer *Aliya* but only the males can go up to read from the Torah. This Hebrew word *Aliyah* translates as *elevation or going up.* It is both used to being called up to the Torah reading and for moving to the land of Israel. Many times I've witnessed Jews who wandered around for years and are coming home and Chabad rabbis give them impromptu bar-mitzvah when they are called for the first time to come up for *Aliyah.*

SIMCHAH TORAH - Dancing with the Torah is the norm of this Holiday. Men both young and old will be seen making a circle around the ***bimah*** to commemorate the last day of the reading of the Torah before we start reading again. If you see me on this day dancing on Lincoln Road, don't think I'm going nuts!. On our last *Simchah Torah*, we lost our friends during the turn to Lincoln road since we must have all been filled with vodka. We were joyously hugging the Torah, singing and dancing as we transferred the scroll to one another for the privilege of carrying it as we made a brief stroll in the streets; we miraculously found our friends back at our synagogue at 669 Lincoln lane. Boys and girls tagged along with their mini-Torah waving flags; we all looked like we just won a soccer match somewhere in Latin America! Who says we Jews don't know how to enjoy life? Liquor as in Grey Goose(TR), Absolut(TR) and Belvedere(TR) and many other brands of vodka are *kosher* and of course were overflowing and not to worry, as usual there was plenty of food as in any Jewish holiday except Yom Kippur.

CHAPTER 14

Bris And Upsherenish - (Will The Boys Have Fun ?)

Bris or brit milah - In Jewish law, although the human soul exists before birth, human life begins at birth. **Judaism completely rejects the notion of original sin**. According to Judaism, a child is born pure, completely free from sin (now you know why I was always drawn to Judaism). I was excited to attend a *Brit milah* for a friend's son not just for the sumptuous food but because of an overwhelming feeling of joy in ushering in a newborn to the tribe that early. I was fascinated by this cycle of life event that it is a big deal that their friends and close family flew in from out of town at such a short notice (7 days) to witness this momentous occasion.

Of all of the commandments in Judaism, the ***brit milah*** (**literally, covenant of circumcision**) is probably the one most universally observed. It is commonly referred to as a **bris** (covenant). Even the most secular of our Jewish friends and acquaintances, who observe no other part of Judaism, almost always observe these laws. Of course, until quite recently, the majority of males in the United States were routinely circumcised, but the ritual of the

brit milah is not merely the process of physically removing the foreskin, and many otherwise non-observant Jews observe the entire ritual. This commandment to circumcise is given at Genesis 17:10-14 and Leviticus 12:3. The covenant was originally made with Abraham, It is the first commandment specific to the Jews.

Like many Jewish commandments, the ***brit milah*** is commonly perceived to be a hygienic measure, however the biblical text states the reason for this commandment quite clearly: *circumcision is an outward physical sign of the eternal covenant between G-d and the Jewish people.*

Bris is performed on the ***eighth day*** of the child's life, during the day. Circumcisions can be performed on *Shabbat* even though they involve the drawing of blood which is ordinarily forbidden on *Shabbat.* The Torah doesn't specify the reason for the eighth day although modern medicine has revealed that an infant's blood clotting mechanism stabilizes on the eighth day after birth. The health benefits of this practice are purely incidental.

Circumcision is performed by a ***mohel*** (a pious, observant Jew educated in the relevant Jewish law and in surgical techniques, circumcision by a regular physician does not qualify as a valid **brit milah**). Various blessings are recited including one over wine and a drop of wine is placed in the child's mouth, then the child is given a formal Hebrew name. As in most Jewish life events, family and friends will gather from different parts of the world to bear witness to this ritual which is followed by a festive meal. In fact, an acquaintance of mine who was not invited to my wedding and unbeknownst to me wanted to grace the occasion made this remark "I hope you will remember to invite me on your son's **bris**".

Upsherenish _ When a *boy turns 3 years* old, he is given his first haircut or **upsherenish** and then begins his Jewish education. During the ceremony, everyone in attendance is invited to snip a lock of the child's hair. I've witnessed 2 of this momentous occasions and watched the transformation of these boys when they were just babies, their hair getting longer and now they are starting to be elevated to the first phase of boyhood and surprisingly, the boys initially were intimidated when the first set of hair were cut but as more family/friends participated, eventually they had fun, and did behave!). Reform or conservative synagogues do not practice this ceremony so you may not get an invitation if you are not in a Chabad or Haredi community.

A child's hair is not cut until age 3 because the Torah compares man to a tree. The root of the ***upsherin*** is a verse in the Torah which compares man to a tree. Just as a tree emerges from a tiny seed to grow tall and bear fruit, so a small child grows in knowledge and bears the fruit of his good deeds. A fruit is not fit for eating until the tree has aged to three years and the first fruits cut after three years are to be brought to G-d as thanks for the success of the crop and the way the child's hair is cut at age 3 is in recognition of G-d's blessing as the child is about to go out and endeavor his Jewish education.

At 3, a child takes a deeper understanding of the world. It is also customary to dip the child's fingers in honey and place them on Hebrew letters, to bring home the sweetness of learning Torah. After the ***upsherenish***, the boy begins to wear a ***kippa*** (**Yamulke or** skullcap) regularly as well as a **tzittzit**. The *kippa* is a skull cap worn by boys and men as a sign of respect for G-d. The *tzitzit* are the fringes worn at the waist, the fringes made of threads and knots that combine to represent the 613 commandments of the Torah. This tradition gives the boy a strong sense of family from the start.

Symbolically, according to the accounts of Deena Yellin[47] on her son's ***upsherenish*** "snipping the baby locks pushes my son towards adulthood and I felt my child moving away from the security of my womb into the larger community. I am comforted, knowing of the small things we can do that are everlasting. We can plant a tree, we can create happy memories. We can pass on a beautiful custom to our children. That after all, is the ultimate gift we can give to our descendants".

As a couple, though we have no children, I can't help but ponder the thought of another beautiful yet simple Jewish custom that fills a child's memories and ultimately his future family with another remarkable tradition that can be passed on to the future generation.

CHAPTER 15

Weddings And Sheva Berachot (The 7 Blessings)

WEDDINGS ARE LIFE CHANGING CEREMONIES in most cultures but I noticed it is even more pronounced in the orthodox Jewish community. Attendance in this very important life cycle event made me appreciate more the beauty of marriage in the context of Judaism. As most of us know, the preparation before weddings can be overwhelming.

My first secular Jewish wedding was an intense 5 months preparation complicated by a new research position at the University of Miami Transplant team so you can just imagine the pre-wedding jitters we went thru. Thankfully, Robert was a true partner in this endeavor, he was responsible for talking to the caterers, searching the venue and many other tasks. We also had to accommodate out of town guests from California, Boston and Switzerland so our wedding day was hectic, my west coast family were taking a leisurely ride on the Pink Lady(TR) tour boat off Bayside on the morning of my wedding and I drove myself to Rusty Pelican(TR) restaurant in Key Biscayne for the wedding and reception.

My brothers and several guests were in awe of the message that our *Reform* rabbi on our first wedding mentioned about the significance of the **chupah,** the seven blessings and breaking the glass to commemorate the destruction of the temple in Jerusalem. But, the phrase that got the most attention from my friends was our rabbi's explanation of *"Therefore a man shall leave his father and mother and cling to his wife, and they shall become one flesh"* as quoted from Parsha Bereishit (Chapter 2:Verse 24; first Parsha of the Torah). Judaism has numerous rules to honor the parents but G-d has special emphasis of the importance of family unity as a priority so it's a clear message for in –laws to give the couple a breather!

My Filipina friends asserted the custom of the ***money***[48] dance practiced in Philippine weddings where cash is pinned on the bride's gown by the wedding guests of the groom and the bride's guests pin money on the groom's suit to help the couple build a nest egg and wish the newlyweds a good fortune· It culminated with the all too familiar Jewish custom of dancing the **Horah** that I slipped and almost fell from the chair! It was so much fun but it was intense and hectic, the following morning, we travelled to Paris for our honeymoon leaving behind our friends and family who flew in from out of town.

The observant Jewish unions, has a more spiritual and logical approach to the unity of bride and groom. It is a one week celebration and definitely allows the couple to bond with close friends and family and provides the bride a week of respite before she takes on her new role in her Jewish home (including meal preparations, laundry, cleaning and other tasks). Don't be surprised of the huge volume of guests (400 or more is very common), because with orthodox weddings, the whole community is invited as in Robert's cousin's wedding in Lakewood, New Jersey, where I saw a sea of men with black hats happily dancing after the ceremony. These wedding receptions are held at extremely large halls to accommodate the many guests and the all night dancing. Men dance with men; women dance with women only: you'll be surprised to see the men's dance moves and twists.

The first week of marriage is celebrated by the newlyweds in a holiday fashion. Holiday finery is worn throughout the week, neither of them goes to work and they are treated royally. This custom originated with the week of festivities which followed the marriage between Jacob and Leah in biblical times.

This week is so called (*Sheva Berachot*) **"Seven Benedictions"** referring to the seven blessings recited following the "Grace after Meals", the same ones recited under the *chuppah* during the wedding, consist of requests for G-ds blessings for the newlywed couple.

Family and close friends divide the honors and they collaborate on each of the **Sheva *Bracho*t**. The meals traditionally feature singing and some words of Torah delivered by the groom, bride or invited guests. After the grace is completed, six guests are invited to take a cup of wine and recite a blessing of *Sheva Brachot.* It is important that there is a *minyan* and that among the guest list, the need for the presence of a "new" face such as someone not present at the wedding or any of the previous **Sheva Brachot** be present. We were once asked to be sure to attend this event and after learning of the rationale, we really appreciated its relevance.

The first is the blessing over the wine since wine has the ability to reveal the person behind the façade, the hidden elements behind ones personality; an appropriate metaphor for marriage, when 2 soul mates resolve to accept each other unconditionally.

The purpose of the second blessing is that the couple declares that their marriage has a higher goal rather than merely satisfying their own needs and desires. All was created for G-d's glory, including and especially the *Jewish home.* The subsequent blessings are for man, woman, Jerusalem, joy and completion and beyond since marriage is when souls of the bride and groom finally reach completion and then use that accomplishment as a springboard to tap into the divine essence of their souls and the world at large.

The blessings have significance and profound meaning and are so thought provoking that I would encourage readers to learn the details and more esoteric rationale for these blessings on Chabad.org.

Nothing says *Jewish wedding* more than the sound of the breaking glass. Depending on whom you ask, this breaking of the glass is a symbol of the destruction of the temple in Jerusalem; a representation of the fragility of human relationships and in a recent biracial wedding we attended of a Chinese groom and Jewish bride; they were reminded by their rabbi that marriage like glass is so fragile that they need to handle it with loving care because once it's broken you can't put it back together! How apropos and true is this statement! Thereafter, guests shouted ***"mazel tov"*** which meant congratulations or good luck and the partying started. I was privileged to welcome the groom to the tribe as well since we had similar backgrounds and he quickly quipped "thank you, I know what you mean".

On our first Jewish wedding, our reform rabbi suggested for us to use a plastic glass to avoid accident, on our orthodox wedding we used real glass and thankfully no accidents occurred.

CHAPTER 16

Shmirah Or Shmurah And What Is A Shivah?

DON'T GET BOGGED DOWN WITH these words since they are literally worlds apart. In Hebrew, just a simple twist of the tongue can change the meaning of the words and most of the time the root words can be deciphered in so many ways.

Shmurah (*watched*) matzot (unleavened flat bread) are round, kneaded and shaped by hand similar to the *matzot* baked by the Children of Israel as they left Egypt; wheat is guarded from the time that it is harvested, the making process must take no more than 18 minutes, after that, the **matzoh** is no longer considered unleavened. It is usually used during the ***Seder*** nights especially on the first night of Passover. Personally, my husband and I prefer the taste of the *Shmurah* matzot, it's artisanal and of course commands a higher price; all *matzohs* are not created equal as you will discern when your Jewish taste buds get sophisticated.

Shmirah (guarding) –Just as there is a way to live as a Jew, there is also a way to be buried as a Jew. In Judaism, a dead body is never to be left alone between the time of death and the time of burial.

It's a tradition called **shmirah,** or guarding, the fundamental message of Judaism about death and bereavement is that *we are not alone.* (Be careful with the pronunciation; I slipped my tongue once hence I know). This task is performed by members of the community's *hevra kadisha*- holy society- who do the watching in the funeral home. However, if this happens during Shabbat, family members will perform the ritual of *shmirah.* First the body is washed, then there is ritual washing before the body is dressed in simple linen shrouds. Members of this holy society prepare bodies for burial according to detailed rituals meant to honor the deceased and preserve their modesty. It is for this reason that Jews prohibit open caskets. Men prepare the bodies of men; women prepare women.

Jewish burials take place as quickly as possible, following the principle of honoring the dead, usually within 24 hours unless there is not enough time due to Shabbat, a holiday or awaiting the arrival of family members such as the recent funeral we attended of Robert's aunt in New Jersey which was delayed awaiting the arrival of Robert's nephew from Israel.

Judaism emphasizes that all are equal in death and Jewish law mandates a simple pine box, the coffin have no metal- even the sides are connected by wooden dowels. The aim is to ensure its complete disintegration, fulfilling the verse from Genesis: "*For you are dust, and to dust you shall return*". Every time we visit the cemetery, the more I respect the value of humility instilled in Judaism as I see the tombstones made of stone or granite, similar to those around it; just with the Hebrew names of the deceased engraved and the dates of death; no mausoleums, no gilded buildings and not above the ground. This makes so much sense to me, we don't need to show off with those expensive, silver or gold plated coffins or mausoleums and ornate buildings to wow the living so others can say uh and ah. (I understand the reasons why other religions or cultures do it).

The funeral service is usually short and family and or close friends could pay tribute of how the deceased lived his life. Once, we went to visit Robert's parents' graves and we noticed a Chabad rabbi waiting to talk to us. It turned out, they were awaiting for a **minyan** (gathering of ten adult men) to bury someone. As soon as Robert came, the son of the deceased introduced himself to Robert and lo and behold, both their parents had done business together in the past when Robert's Dad owned a light bulb supply store in Coral Gables. After the burial service, I turned to Robert and said 'there was a reason why we have been postponing the gravesite visit for a few weeks; what you do in life still affects you even in death, because this episode is a good example of how we are connected to people in our past; in life and in death". Hashem had arranged for Robert to be the tenth man for this burial; Robert remembered the woman's husband as an honest and respectful business partner and friend of his father. Sometimes, family members may hear good deeds unbeknownst to them that was performed by their loved ones and these could get revealed during this service. By the way, dirt is shoveled on top of the grave in performance of a *chesed shel emet- a true act of kindness-* **seeing the vessel of a soul is honorably and properly buried-** because it is something that cannot be repaid.

Shiva (literally means seven) is the week long mourning period after the funeral of a close friend or relative. Helping a family during their grieving process by providing them home cooked meals or arranging for meals to be sent to their house is another simple yet kind gesture in Jewish communities specially in close communities. It is never a tradition to send flowers or wreaths, instead Jews use that money to take care of the living such us donating to a charity designated by the family or helping those who are in pain and suffering.

"The rituals of death teach us how to live more meaningful lives; as religions go, Judaism is far more concerned about what happens in *this world than the world to come, Jewish rituals can serve not only to sanctify the dead, but also to humanize* the *living.* When so much in modern life is outsourced, there is something clarifying, maybe even purifying, about witnessing a loved one's final days. In caring for someone after death, and being expected to take part in rituals at once deeply uncomfortable and comforting, Judaism forces us to examine our own lives and deeds- and to ask ourselves: "Are we putting our own vessels to their best use?". (Barry Weiss, Wall Street Journal, March 17, 2016).

How Jews value life and treat the dead are some of the most profound, sapient and deeply insightful aspects of Judaism that I esteem. I can't fathom how my life would be NOT being a Jewish woman. I have the confidence to live a Jewish life and yet I retain profound humility for my limitations. It makes me introspect deeply in my daily life of where I am and where am I going....???

CHAPTER 17

Chanukah - Illuminating The World

I OFTEN WONDER WHAT MY imprint will be in this world? People come and go and when I visit old historical cities like Savannah, Georgia in America and cities in Europe such as at Dubrovnik, Croatia and Tomar, Portugal; I am often enchanted by the compelling Jewish pioneers who carved amazing lives and impacted their societies in many incredible ways. I can't help but reflect on the influences that many people are oblivious to such accomplishments specially if they are not interested in Jewish history.

The Talmud states that *the people of Israel were exiled amongst nations only so that converts maybe added to them.* In the most basic level, this is a reference to those non- Jews who, in the centuries of Jewish dispersion, have come in contact with the Jewish people and decided to convert to Judaism, and I am one of them. The Talmud is also referring to the many other souls which Jews have transformed and elevated in the course of Jewish exile "*the sparks of holiness*" contained within the physical creation. The great Kabbalist, Rabbi Isaac Luria taught that "every created entity has a spark of Godliness within it, a pinpoint of divinity that constitutes its soul such as its spiritual function and design. And when we utilize something to serve the creator, we penetrate its shell of mundanity, revealing and realizing its divine essence".

One of the most famous temporary attractions in December to tourists on Lincoln road in Miami Beach is our friend Roger Abramson's large **Chanukah menorah** made of shells. This is the best time to visit this eclectic artwork, a stand out in this famous street in Miami Beach, not just for the free hot **latkes (**potato pancakes**)** and jelly doughnuts served to everyone who wants it but to partake in the candle lighting ceremony starting with one candle lit up together with the head candelabra, gradually increasing nightly until the 8th candle is lighted. The festive atmosphere, Klezmer music and a chance for kids to spin the oversized shell **dreidl** is unique, thanks to our own Chabad of Miami Beach also known as Chabad on Wheels. We have made a ritual out of this and we always invite our Bagel and *Pancit* club group to attend the ceremony to help brighten this world with good deeds or mitzvahs and of course pictures are eagerly shared on Facebook! (*see photos*) and we certainly generate lots of "likes" for our magnificent photos.

In my trip to Manila in 2008, I was surprised to see a ceramic candelabra that looked like what we had back in Florida displayed in a store near Malate so my curiosity was peeked and my fact finding conversation with the owner/ manager who excitedly asked me " have you shopped from a Spiegel catalogue?" I said yes, and he confirmed they're one of the many Jewish business clients where they export their goods. Now I know how Philippine made candelabras and kiddush wine cups found their way at a Judaica store in Miami Beach. Nowadays, I find it fascinating to see Filipino-Jewish connections everywhere.

Many Filipinos and Jews are not aware that we have a strong Jewish connection in our history as well. The history of the Jewish[49] community in Manila goes back to the Spanish Inquisition when many Jews of Spain were forcibly converted to Christianity. The first island of the Philippines sighted by the Spanish expedition of Ferdinand Magellan in 1521 after having left the Mariana Islands was Samar. Known as " *Marranos*", they accompanied Spanish adventurers who settled in the Far Eastern ports, particularly in Northern Samar. One of the first recorded Jews to have arrived, reaching Manila in the 1590's were Jorge and Domingo Rodriguez[50] who were tried and convicted in Mexico city because the inquisition was not operating in the Philippines. Many references also mentioned *Marranos* entering the island of Samar and that Samar island may have been named after *Samaria. Isla de Batang* is the first land mass you will see after a long travel in the Pacific Ocean going to Manila and is part of the Galleon Trade route and home of the ancient shipbuilding industry. (Samar island is adjacent to my province of Leyte, connected by the beautiful San Juanico bridge; which was also devastated by super typhoon Haiyan or Yolanda).

The first permanent settlement of Jews during the Spanish colonial years began with the arrival of three Levy brothers from Alsace- Lorraine who escaped the aftermath of the Franco-Prussian War in 1870. As entrepreneurs, their business ventures over the years included jewelry retail, general merchandizing and import trade in gems, pharmaceuticals and automobiles. The Levy brothers were joined by Turkish, Syrian and Egyptian Jews.

A Syrian- Jewish trader, A.N. Hashim[51], helped Filipino national hero, Dr. Jose Rizal, escape from *Dapitan* (place in Mindanao where J. Rizal was exiled from 1892-1896) . He also established the Manila Grand Opera house and later diversified into government supply and contracting for both the U.S. and Filipino governments, mining, and import-export businesses.

Michael Goldenberg was another notable and successful of the early Manila Jews. Born in Singapore in 1889, his father was Dr. Leon Goldenberg, a captain in the French Army medical corps. Dr. Goldenberg had moved his family to Manila in 1894 and managed a pharmacy on Escolta Avenue. He became friends with several of the **Katipuneros** (*members of a secret organization that led to the outbreak of the Philippine revolution in 1896*) and reportedly served as a conduit for Marcelo H. del Pilar (one of the Filipino heroes).

At age 7, Michael Goldenberg witnessed Jose Rizal's execution (the Philippines' national hero) that changed his life. He went on to become one of the most ardent Rizalists and translated several of Rizal's works from Spanish into English. His *Rizaliana* collection is one of the most valuable and extensive in pre-war Manila.

Michael Goldenberg founded an import-export firm specializing in textiles, and in 1920, opened Goldenberg's department store. They bought a historic residence on Calle General Solana, which came to be called the Goldenberg mansion. *The*

Goldenberg mansion served as General Arthur MacArthur's home and headquarters during his tenure as American Military governor of the Philippines from 1900-1901 and hosted the first session of the Philippine senate in 1916. The Marcos administration apparently acquired the mansion in 1960's and annexed it as part of the Malacanang Presidential Palace.

Many Jews also came to the Philippines as members of the US military in the campaign to pacify the Philippines. Among the 70,000 US troops were a number of American Jews who stayed in the Philippines at the end of their tour of duty. Notable among them was John M. Switzer, who was a classmate of Herbert Hoover at Stanford University. Some came as civilian businessmen charged with supplying the American forces.

During the American period, servicemen from the American military decided to remain in the islands and became permanent residents.They were joined by Jewish teachers from the United States who also arrived with a contingent of "*Thomasites*", volunteer teachers who gave instruction to Filipino children. Jewish businessmen set up shops in the Philippines and extended businesses from the US mainland. Two of those names were Emil Bachrach and Morton I. Netzorg. Mr. Bachrach built a sizable commercial empire from private cars to taxi services, became Director of the People's Bank and helped organize the Philippines' first airline. He was a generous philanthropist and supported both Jewish and Christian causes. The synagogue and cultural hall which the family financed, bore his name. By 1918, the Jewish community totaled 150 and included Russian Jews who escaped the Bolshevik Revolution.

Manuel Luis Quezon[52] was elected President of the Philippine Commonwealth in 1935. In the pre-war era, he developed a personal and political relationship with Paul. V. McNutt, the US High Commissioner to the Philippines as well as with many influential members of the Jewish community. He actively supported the Jewish refugee program, expressing his willingness to help secure visas for up to ***a million Jewish immigrants***, but American officials squelched such a large number, fearing the Philippines would be used as a backdoor entry to the United States. He even proposed an ambitious plan for over 50,000 Jews to found a settlement in Mindanao, in the southern part of the Philippines. (I could just imagine the development of the southern part of the Philippines if this materialized, would the violent Jihadist group *Abbu Sayyaf* been able to take hold ? Undaunted, Quezon donated personal real estate for a group home and working farm (a kibbutz, although Quezon did not call it that) outside Manila in Marikina.

Kristallnacht galvanized many Jews into action, spurring them to make painful decision to leave home and seek safety abroad. With the passage of the Tydings-McDuffie Act, also known as the Philippine Independence Act in 1935, Filipinos were subjected to severe immigration quotas. As the situation became dire in Europe, increasing numbers of Jews searched with greater urgency and in 1938, the first group of Jewish refugees arrived in Manila from Shanghai.

Manila Jewry *(Manilaners)* included Dr. Herbert Zipper[53] who was an inmate at Dachau and started a secret orchestra and composed the music for the song *Dachau Lied*, and went on to become the director of the Manila Symphony. He founded the

Brooklyn Symphony Orchestra in 1946 and upon his move to Chicago, founded the Music Center of the North Shore in Winnetka, Illinois and the National Guild of Community Music schools which promotes music education. Upon his move to Los Angeles in 1972, he became the projects director of the School of Performing Arts of the University of California at Los Angeles. (A short documentary film in 1995 entitled Never Give Up: 20th century Odyssey of Herbert Zipper was nominated for best documentary at the Oscars). Mr. Zipper had joined his fiancée Trudl Dubsky[54], a Viennese ballerina who had fled earlier and set up the dance program at the University of the Philippines. (The Colburn Dance Institute at the University of Southern California was renamed Trudl Zipper[55] Dance Institute in 2008).

Other prominent *Manilaners* were the Frieder[56] brothers from Cincinnati who owned the Helena Cigar Factory in the Philippines, who raised money, secured affidavits, visas and jobs for Jewish refugees from Europe. Siegfried Strausser, a German Jew and expert cigar maker from Schweinfurt, Germany with his wife Klara was one of the 1200 German and Austrian Jews who managed to flee the Nazis.

These episodes in the journey of Jews to the Philippines who escaped the holocaust were well documented by Mr. Frank Ephraim, one of the refugees and a witness to humanitarian efforts of former President Manuel L. Quezon's efforts to save European Jewry in his book " *Escape to Manila*[57]*: From Nazi Tyranny to Japanese Terror*".

Alfred Weinstein, another Manilaner[58], was a Harvard-educated medical doctor, who volunteered to fight in the Pacific specifically because he did not want to be taken prisoner in the European theater. He served as a field surgeon during the Philippine campaign, retreating with the Fil-American troops down the Bataan peninsula. He survived the *Bataan Death March* and 3 ½ years in the Japanese POW camps of the Philippines. Noel Izon and Sharon Delmendo's film "*An Open Door*" is a wealth of information of the historical perspective of Jewish presence in the Philippines[59].

In the 1950's Jack Nasser[60] (not to be confused with Jacques Nasser, the former Ford motor executive) and his brothers established a textile manufacturing plant in the Philippines which grew into the largest textile factory in the country. He came from a family of Syrian immigrants who left Aleppo to Israel then to the Philippines. He also founded *Philexcel*, a real estate development business. Mr. Nasser assisted the Philippine government in the conversion of the former U.S. Air Force Clark air base into the Clark Freeport where now currently more than 800 companies operate within the zone that include telecommunications, hotels and leisure resorts in Angeles city, Pampanga. In March, 2016 our Miami based Brazilian artist Romero Britto opened the Jack R. Nasser collection of the Philexcel Art Center (philexcel.com). Mr. Nasser collected over 100 paintings and numerous sculptures from Filipino artists representing the *Mabini Art genre*, a Philippine art form once disparaged by local patrons but which of late has been receiving much deserved appreciation. The center is a dynamic fulcrum for contemporary art in Central Luzon with free public access.

The Open Doors Monument was unveiled in Rishon Lezion near Tel Aviv in 2009 in recognition of the Philippines' humanitarian support for Jews. The Philippines Open Door Policy during World War II has saved between 1200 to 2000 Jews during World War II (different sources vary in the exact number of Jews saved). Let us not forget, that the Philippines was one of 33 countries who voted in favor of UN Resolution 181 that paved the way for Israel's independence in 1948.

As of this writing, I am aware of the existence of 5 synagogues in the Philippines. The synagogue in De La Costa Ave in Makati is conservative- orthodox and is conveniently located near the heart of the business center. The Chabad Manila/Makati is on *Kalayaan* street and they are in the process of constructing an 8 story building in Makati and Chabad Cebu is in an apartment where the rabbi and his family live on Pres. Aguinaldo street. Chabad Philippines is under the leadership of Rabbi Levy of Manila whose wife is from North Miami Beach. A fourth Chabad synagogue just opened in El Nido, Palawan in Dec. 2016, to service the regular influx of international tourists visiting the spectacular, sparkling white sand beaches and diving resorts of the island.

It may behoove Filipinos to learn that Mike Hanopol[61], the Filipino guitarist and rocker of my generation (70-80's) will be ordained as the first Filipino rabbi in 2016. He migrated to the US in 1982 and was introduced to his father's Jewish relatives in New York where he also learned his family left the pogroms of Kiev, Russia in the 1920's.

I will refrain from discussing the different Jewish history of Asian cities such as Japan and India who have significant histories, but let me indulge about China just a bit.

Shanghai is a very vibrant city and without studying history, it was difficult for me and my husband on our visit in 2014 to imagine that along the Bund, where Shanghai's prominent buildings are located such as the elegant Peace Hotel (where the rich and famous of China converged for their soirees in the 1800's) were once owned by Jewish real estate magnates; the Sassoon family, considered the Rothschilds of the East, who at some time owned 1,800+ buildings in Shanghai area. His family were also responsible for helping feed the Jews who escaped the Nazi's when Shanghai hosted approximately 20,000 Jews including the well-known *Meir Yeshiva* students of Latvia.

We may never discern the hands of G-d but we can infer that Jewish dispersion definitely had influenced mankind even in the far corners of Asian cities such as in the Philippines and China.

CHAPTER 18

Our Jewish Home

I AM NOT THE SUM of my free-spirited collective past; I am a breathing, constantly evolving,dynamic human being, eager to embrace the future. I welcome opportunities to refine myself and whatever catapults me to live a joyful and extraordinary life. I am cognizant and fully accept the repercussions of my decision to follow the Jewish faith and way of living. Personal growth and enlightenment has always been a quest of mine, or it could be that my soul was restless until it found the *Jewish home*?

We belong to an exclusive club; the *Bagel* and *Pancit (Philippine noodles)* club where our delectable *kosher* style Filipino specialties are commonly served when we get together and reflect our group, a racial mix of Jewish men with Filipina wives. Fittingly our motto was: *Next year in Manila or Jerusalem* .Our experiences, challenges and memories are unique to our group being married to nice Jewish boys and this mini group were the usual guests at cycle of life celebrations; leaned on each other and discussed matters that other Filipina friends not married to the tribe will not comprehend.

A good friend made a tradition of hosting Dec. 24 parties so we can all share in the festivities where Jews and gentiles gather together and we make the most of the holidays. We try to be creative in December because we understand that some of us get homesick and unless it's Sabbath, we generally grace this occasion to be with friends, if it falls on a Sabbath, occasionally I hosted it at home.

The same circle of friends were invited to *Seders*, *Rosh Hoshana* gathering or breaking the fast post *Yom Kippur* and graced special occasions of Bar and Bat Mitzvahs. Thankfully, for a few years, our friend Divina hosted the elegant and much sought after second night Passover and *Rosh Hoshana* yearly dinners and we've watched the evolution of the topic du jour from bar/bat mitzvah preparation to engagements and currently weddings of their children.

My husband and I spearhead attendance at ***menorah*** (candelabrum with branches used during the festival of *Chanukah*) lighting ceremonies in Miami Beach or other major holidays, thereby bringing our friends to the fold; they didn't come just to see a famous movie director, who occasionally was a featured guest to light the shell menorah on Lincoln Road. Our group runs the gamut of level of observance, but as we experienced at Chabad, the rabbis are non-judgmental, warm and very welcoming hence the positive experiences reinforce us to come for more social activities and enhance our deeper understanding of Judaism.

I was not oblivious of the fact that there has to be an education that will enhance one's personal happiness, achieve our life's mission and benefit society as well. I can see the difference in my own transformation and road to enlightenment because of what I learned from the Torah with the building of character as a primary focus especially the refinement of one's moral and ethical values. I strongly believe it should be part of everyone's learning process.

Every morning upon awakening, we wash our hands to thank G-d for restoring our soul and be truly grateful for our physical existence. I give thanks daily for keeping me alive, truly this is the relationship I want to start (with Hashem) in the morning for I know that as the day goes by, despite the frenzy of chores, events and excitement, I feel I have a backbone that will be there for me hence I share my first hour with *Him*. Don't we always share our first bite of a scrumptious cake with our loved one?

The most beautiful sight to behold is watching my husband perform **tefilin** every morning (except Yom Tov days); he learned to rearrange his schedule so that he has time to perform this ritual, again, it is not coerced but done on his own volition.

Call me traditional or whatever, but I relish cooking and preparing creative, healthy meals for my husband although sometimes I spoil him (and me) with cookies and fiber rich cakes using organic ingredients for our Shabbat or to share with his colleagues at work. Unlike most couples, we have hours to talk about how our day unfolded, what our plans are for the next few days and exchange ideas on different aspects of our lives including our future. As the Jewish sages declared, *man receives sustenance only through the merit of his wife; happiness, blessing, goodness and protection come from the wife.*

Many articles have been written about the advantages of families eating meals together. Miriam Weinstein in her book "*The surprising Power of Family Meals*[62]" mentioned the magic bullet that would improve the quality of a family's daily life, children's chances of success and family health. When sharing a meal together, family bonds become stronger, children are better adjusted, family members eat more nutritional meals, less likely to be overweight and abuse alcohol or drugs. For younger children, having a routine family meal can provide a sense of security and a feeling of belonging. How much more for a festive atmosphere during Shabbat, teenage angst can be calmed and a lively discussion for parents and children to catch up with each other can fill the Shabbos table!

Since we have no children, Robert usually puts the coins on the *Tzedakah* box while I'm preparing the oil lamp candelabra. I can't help but think of the habits formed by children giving *Tzedakah* before *shabbat*, women's mitzvah of lighting candles on Friday night, *kashrut* observance and remembering the **613 mitzvots**! This is the response to peoples' dilemma regarding organized religion, we **do need a compass** to a life with a mission and the Torah is our guide.

Baking challah to me is a spiritual transformation; making this bread bridges this world with the world of the divine. I was not much of a baker, initially I rationalized that buying store bought *Kosher challah* would serve the same purpose and my husband and I devour the bread instantly on *Shabbos* but after many classes of challah baking that I had attended, I was determined to make them at home. Now, I get very excited to knead the dough and bake them; it is not an obligation but rather a personal expression of transforming a physical object to a way of connecting with G-d and I actually look forward to it. I can tell you the big difference in taste and flavor when it is home- made and how much more for children when they come home on Friday afternoon welcomed by the aroma of fresh baked challah that will surely be imprinted in their memories for generations.

It's true, we have missed many Olympic opening ceremonies on Friday evenings from London to Rio de Janeiro in 2016, (did we really miss anything....alright.... probably the famous catwalk of a supermodel as the girl from Ipanema?). The serenity, peace and contemplative time for enjoyment with family, unencumbered by distractions of the television grew on us that my husband even lamented that he wished he had more of this quality time with his parents on *Shabbat.* We have 25 hours to truly enjoy and savor our meals together leisurely with dessert, tea or coffee and be with each other, read religious books and magazines in the afternoon or take a few hours of a much coveted *Shabbos* nap! Robert lovingly calls me his *Shabbos and kosher* police because I am the one who makes sure that we light our Shabbat candles on time but he's also delighted when I remind him to have our favorite organic chocolate ice cream after lunch before we have a meat dish for dinner!

Through the Torah, G-d has given Jews commandments *to put G-d as the center of our universe, ask for forgiveness and offer gratitude daily.* Like most Jews all over the world, every morning immediately upon awakening I recite the blessing *"Modeh Ani Lefanecha, Melech Chai Vekayon, Shehechezarta Bi Nishmati Bechemla, Raba Emuanatecha"* as I ritually wash my hands. Translated in English as "I offer thanks to You, living and eternal King, for You have mercifully restored my soul within me; Your faithfulness is great". Lord our G-d, the Lord is one" - a declaration of faith, a pledge of allegiance **to One God.**

Before retiring every night, we recite the prayer that states "Master of the universe! I hereby forgive anyone who has angered or vexed me, or sinned against me, either physically or financially, against my honor or anything else that is mine, whether accidentally or intentionally, inadvertently or deliberately, by speech or by deed; may no man be punished on my account". The lessons of forgiveness, gratitude, compassion and believing that G-d, Creator or Master of the Universe will provide what we ask for are lessons I learned as well from author and lecturer Christie Sheldon's Love and Above programs and the interrelationship I discern fascinates me that these sagacious insights can be found in the Torah that has guided and enlightened generations of rabbis and Jews and the difference is that with information technology, more are revealed, expounded and shared to the whole world.

Aside from volunteering monthly as support staff/mentors of young adults with special needs or feeding the homeless on Thanksgiving or Christmas day at the Jewish Federation or at Chapman Community Partnership in downtown Miami; we got involved with a visionary project about this non-government organization (NGO) from Israel that provided a duplicable and sustainable assistance to Haitian farmers helping them from the grounds up after the devastating earthquake.

This is an endeavor that my husband and I are extremely proud of at this time because this partnership proverbially *teaches people how to fish* which is my motto when doing charitable giving. We were determined to assist in any small way we can after typhoon Haiyan or locally known as Yolanda; wreaked havoc, ruined farms and families and left thousands of people dead. I had a burning desire to do something to improve their lives when I came back to visit my home province of Leyte. My city of *Baybay* was not severely affected so we decided to collaborate with IsraAid staff (www.IsraAid.co.il) whom I knew were in Ormoc city which is a half hour by car from my place. Our perseverance paid off in our desperate search to find a representative and we finally met Ms. Adva Vilchinski who was then the Philippines' country director for *IsraAid* and happened to be staying a block from our hotel at Century city in Makati. We had a scrumptious dinner at an Israeli restaurant called Benny's Falafel(TR) then discussed what we can do to contribute to this NGO.

My husband "a Jew from Miami and his wife, a Filipina from Leyte" apparently appealed to the board of directors hence we took the role of fundraisers for the agricultural restoration project thru a crowd funding platform called Global Giving. This was doubly meaningful to me since my father was the former regional director for the Bureau of Soils (Ministry of Agriculture) covering Leyte and Samar and his job then entailed soil analysis and guidance to farmers in improving farming techniques. We embarked on this project with no fund-raising experience and managed to get a number of donors (www.globalgiving.org/17225). Even my oldest brother Adrian stated "well, I trust your Israel based NGO so I prefer to give our family and friends' donation to your project". That was a revelation!

We assisted to integrate the work of *IsraAid* with administrators of the Visayas State University (VSU) where my father first taught as an instructor after obtaining his Bachelors in Agronomy from the University of the Philippines. Collaboration is underway with soil and scientific analysis, crop management and post-harvest practices; local governments in Leyte are also recipients of their training programs. They have a partnership with Energy Development Corporation who had decided to invest in locally produced protective structures according to the design based from Israel and there is a plan to build a dam at the water source to meet the water demand. One of the VSU agricultural graduates who hails from this farming community was sent to Israel for training as well. The current update of this project is that the yield of the vegetables and crops has magnified seven fold and better marketing strategies are implemented. (www.globalgiving.org/ *Philippine Agricultural Economic Restoration).*

We still have a *GRAND* vision for projects to be expanded to families such as backyard gardens and connect families to their land and take pride in organic/natural farming that could provide healthy food sources for local residents, provide income and improve independence and self – worth. Education and mentorship are in the horizons.

On my trip to Israel, I was in awe of how every inch of the land was utilized and such a small country with not too friendly neighboring countries (to say the least) could manage to export agricultural products but then again I have no doubts; the Jewish National Fund has a motto that is so apropos that states; ***"If we can make the Desert bloom, the impossible will just take a little longer".***

IsraAid has made significant inroads to the local governments who are excited to expand their efforts to educate more farmers in Leyte and the organization is committed to stay until 2018. This NGO has done an incredible job including the construction of a school in Ipil, Ormoc city; provided fishing boats for fishermen and taught resilience in the community thru their psychosocial counselling of families and collaborated with local businesses (Cebu Pacific Air(TR)) and other governments (Japan and Czechoslovakia) to improve the lives of many Filipino families.

Reading the Facebook(TR) comments of my high school classmates about an upcoming reunion in the Philippines made me introspect deeply how much I have evolved over the years. The friendship we shared and the adventures we had are imprinted in our memories but our lives took different paths. I couldn't help but reflect that I can't partake of *lechon* (roasted whole pig) which is the star of any Filipino feast and neither can I share **kumbaya** with **treif** dishes of crabs, shrimps and everything with pork in them such as eggrolls or our famous pork *adobo.* At our last gathering in April, 2014; I treated them to dishes made of chicken, fish, fresh *lumpia* and other kosher style delicacies. Over the years, here in America I have made new friends exposed to Jewish culture and therefore more tolerant; back home, there are a few who are aware and curious, but a significant amount are critical and intolerant of my conversion. It is my quest that we can still co-exist peacefully and bridge our differences through the common bonds we've shared in the past. I may now be a JAP (*Jewish American Pinay)* but I am cognizant that my past was part and parcel of who I am now and helped shape me as I have moved forward and departed from my juvenile exuberance.

Our house as in most Jewish homes is overflowing with books on Judaism, travel books and magazines of a wide variety. Did I say we have travel books? Yes, because aside from having a wandering soul, I married someone who has wandering soles like me. We share a passion for walking on historical places and soaking in the cultures of the past generations and reimagine how this civilization evolved and at which café a famous writer's *ouvr e* was penned, was it at Café Le Fleur in Paris(TR) or was it at Café Les Deux Magots(TR) where Gertrude Stein or Picasso and friends shared their geniuses?

On our sojourn to Dubrovnik, Croatia, we joined 40 other curious tourists in our bus as we visited the old synagogue that is being revitalized by a Jewish benefactor from New York. I often reflect upon how Jews in their often myriad ways are bound to their history, identity and people in their innate desires to support synagogues or revive old Jewish communities. Their ingenuity is so remarkable as well as the pragmatic ways they implement programs as evidenced by the popular Shabbat dinners they hold at the Jewish ghettos in Venice, Italy. These stories are repeated throughout the many ancient communities with previously large Jewish population including certain cities of Portugal. They have genuine concern for members of the tribe. Kosher food is available almost everywhere there's a Chabad emissary from Malta to Manila. At our summer vacation in Charleston, South Carolina we ate at Hyman's(TR) seafood restaurant which is not a kosher establishment but has *kosher* food prepared by the Chabad of Mt. Pleasant, South Carolina, available for purchase where I was told by the proprietor that they serve about a dozen kosher meals a day.

Judaism has influenced our way of living in so many ways. Years ago, we had put in a contract to purchase a house in Miami Beach but told the realtor that we need to finalize it before the period of **TishB'Av** since I learned from a Jewish women's class that contracts should not be made at this period of mourning of the destruction of the temple in Jerusalem and other sad events in Jewish history. Our seller was not too happy and asked her observant brother about this dilemma we had and needless to say, we got saved because our realtor later found out that there was a structural defect that would have cost us at least $50,000 to repair!

Robert is ecstatic that he is progressing from a conservative/ Rosh Hashana and Yom Kippur Jew to a **tefilin** wrapping, Shabbat observant member of the tribe with a **kosher** home and the **real kosher mezuzas** at the door. As the Chabad rabbis' repeated mantra of "*just do one more mitzvah at a time*" resonate slowly, we are evolving organically. Sometimes with trepidation, mostly with ***jewbilation,*** together we are truly enjoying our spiritual journey the Hasidic way (learning curves and all). Setbacks do happen in each family and weathering life's roadblocks strengthens "team Grand". We are cognizant that **Shalom bayit** or peace at home is similar to observing the Torah.

When we need blessings and guidance we find ourselves sending emails to the **Ohel**[63]of the Rebbe, Menachem Mendel Schneerson, O.B.M., asking him to intercede in our behalf. We had so many successes thru this endeavor and I know that he had helped not only Jews but gentiles as well from the stories I've read such as the *American Pharoah's*[64] jockey who won the elusive triple crown after he visited the Rebbe's ohel in Queens, New York in June, 2015.

I adhere to these character traits from **A to G** to usher a joyful and meaningful life which I am excited to share with you.

Attitude- Have a positive attitude in life, look at life half full rather than half empty. A negative attitude can break you but a positive one can make you.

Beatitude- Be in state of utmost bliss; grace, divine joy; supreme blessedness; learn to send blessings not only to yourself but to others daily.

Compassion-Endeavor to move beyond indifference and judgement. This is essential in order to support each other in the community including genuine concern for the environment. Compassion also means no **Lashon Hara** (gossip).

Determination- Possess a firmness of purpose and resolve to achieve a goal despite obstacles. Sometimes we may have to crawl, jump or break a wall to get what we want.

Ebullience- Have a bubbly enthusiasm or excitement in anything you do in life. This will make life rosy, help uplift others and make your ordinary day a great one.

Fortitude- Possess courage, resilience, strength of mind, character, grit and **chutzpah!**

G-d centered life, Gratitude and Give Back- Acknowledge the source of all being and know that your existence has a spiritual purpose unique to you. Be thankful and grateful daily of what we have as well as what we are given, warts and all. Give back to yourself (*love yourself first*), to your family and to your community and the society at large since we are all interconnected.

Definitely, Judaism has transformed me and I am also aware that in this extraordinary adventure of mine, I have left some people behind. I now focus on what contributions I can do to leave my mark in this world. I may just be an ordinary humming bird who carries hopes for love, joy and celebration. It's delicate grace reminds us that life is rich, beauty is everywhere and every personal connection has meaning and that laughter is life's sweetest creation. I hope that beautiful flowers will bloom later from the seeds of kindness, love and compassion I distributed and will spread along the way.

CHAPTER 19

Jewish Perspectives

Who am I? I am no Elie Wiesel O.B.M., I'm just a perpetual student of Torah who deeply believes in its teachings and the moral values that it instills that has enriched my life in myriad ways. The proverbial phrase "it takes one candle to light a room" inspires me. If I can spark one soul then I have achieved the mission to "love your brother as yourself" as clearly imbued in the Torah.

Here in America, we enjoy religious, economic, political, social and tremendous other blessings. Having lived here most of my life now, I occasionally take these blessings for granted, although my trips to the Philippines keep me grounded. The economic disparity of the population and rampant poverty among Filipinos reminds me to appreciate the abundance we have in this country.

Baila Olidort in her Chabad International editorial[65] noticed the striking contrast between Jews in the former Soviet union and most American Jews. "The former, denied their identity, afraid or too ignorant to pass ***Yiddishkeit*** along to their children, now work hard to make up for the lost years, often beginning with the basics late in life as they try to reclaim their Jewish identity". She reflected on an inspiring event with rueful irony while in attendance at a ribbon cutting for a **brit- mila** or circumcision clinic at a Jewish community complex in Moscow. "Happy to know that they're ***Jewish*** and upon learning that ***brit milah*** is rudimentary to Jewish identity… men whose parents did not circumcise them at 8-days often come forward on their own to have a **bris** and these men were not necessarily observant Jews. I couldn't help but notice the striking contrast between the bright, animating clarity they exuded, and the obfuscation plaguing Americans today. Liberated from fighting for any meaningful cause or calling, some are looking – in all the wrong places, it seems--- to fill the empty time on their hands, reinventing self, family and identity with arbitrary fictions and new narratives. And the more absurd, the more celebrated….."

How does one develop moral character in this vainglorious age of the "**selfie**?" Ethics and virtues are inculcated thru direct and indirect teaching, practiced daily and observed thru actions or inactions in our family and community. Ms. Olidort continued that "it's a question that has been variously explored by the ancients. Some find the answer in the study of stellar role models and time spent in contemplation, spiritual exercises and self-scrutiny. But…, ***the Jewish perspective has always been a practical one: activities of the mind do not necessarily translate into action. Reading the great moral philosophers and pondering the finer points of the virtuous life may inspire a desire to improve oneself. But the timber of moral character is forged in the crucible of hard work and practiced habits".***

I can attest to the difference in discipline that my Torah women's group observed when we visited the girls day school; *Bais*

Chana in Brooklyn. There was an aura of discipline and character with those young girls. The structure and priorities are so different from secular schools, in the observant world, a personal and meaningful connection with G-d is instilled early in life and their role as future Jewish wives and mothers is clearly part of the preparation, girls in their teens are already coordinating or assisting in the different programs at Chabad, whereas in the secular world, priorities are geared towards material or financial success and purposeful or meaningful relationship with our creator is secondary if that even exists.

Oftentimes among family, friends and colleagues, after their children's successes of acceptance at Ivy league universities or for that matter, succeed financially in their chosen careers, some of them have admitted to a lack of a sense of direction in their lives, except sometimes looking forward to the next exotic vacation, planned car purchase or house upgrade. They acknowledge a feeling of losing an important ***mission*** or feel empty when their children move on and they struggle to search for real meaning and purpose in their existence; they feel lost and the common question is **"what's next or where to ?".**

Brotherly love is axiomatic to Judaism and is oft repeated in **Pirkei Avot**, or Ethics of our Fathers- one of the most cited of Jewish texts with maxims such as " If I am only for myself, who am I?". It is also the implacable call of the Rebbe, Menachem Mendel Schneerson O.B.M. " **What matters most, above all else, are our actions- the things we actually do. And we can never do enough.**" As the Lubavitcher Rebbe said " We can fill our time with unlimited content, or waste it away, and the very same unit of time may mean an infinity to one or shrink to nothingness to another. Its true measure varies in direct proportion to what is achieved in it".

Viktor Frankl, author of **Man's Search for Meaning**[66] stated "Don't aim at success. The more you aim at it and make it a target, the more you are going to miss it. For success, like happiness, cannot be pursued; it must ensue, and it only does so as the unintended side effect of one's **personal dedication to a cause greater than oneself**. Listen to what your conscience commands you to do and go on to carry it out to the best of your knowledge. **Those who have a "why" to live, can bear with almost any "how".**

Conversion to Judaism has no end, it may have a beginning but to me, the process is infinite. There is so much to learn and my thirst for it grows deeper that I once told a rabbi that I might be 90 years old before I can be as observant as he is of the *mitzvot* and other practices. To my relief, he calmed me down and said "the good thing is you are doing a *mitzvot* daily; you're going up at your own volition, you're improving in your spiritual height . Acceptance was not an issue although it is inevitable that I can feel doubts from the comments or questions about my sincerity both from the Jewish and Christian community. I was excited but a bit nervous of failing because I didn't speak Hebrew (I've attended several classes, it's not sticking to me yet but Hebrew is in my bucket list, I always refer to the back pages of the Siddur book for translation !).

I was told 3 days before my conversion in December, 2004 that we're supposed to have a wedding ceremony that evening! (OMG!). The head rabbi of the ***beit din*** (3-man rabbinic court) asked me profound questions and he then **"welcomed me to the**

tribe". The ritual immersion in a *mikvah* literally caused an internal metamorphosis in me that is surreal to explain... my life will never be the same.... I chose the Hebrew name of **Chaya** (life). Yes, we managed to have a simple but meaningful wedding ceremony attended by close friends and family at the rabbi's residence.

As a Jewish woman, I am proud to carry the torch of what Yanky Tauber at Chabad.org had expounded regarding the essence of a Jew's existence when he said " What is expected of us, mortal and fragile men? Human beings, hewn of spirit and matter, is a synthesis of the celestial and the animal. Man is empowered to make heaven on earth, to make holy an adjective of land. This is the essence of the divine objective of creation and the mission entrusted to Jews at Mt Sinai; **"to build a dwelling for G-d in the lowly realms, to imbue our plowing, sowing and commerce with a holy and G-dly purpose. The eternal lesson of the Torah's account of the incident of the Spies is to *not allow the wisdom, sensitivity and inspiration of your youth to remain an isolated period in your life. Do not allow your moments of attachment to G-d each* morning to remain a miracle with no bearing on the natural course of your day. Cross into the land, but do not leave your spiritual childhood behind. Remember, that the purpose of it all, is to make your life and the world a Holy Land."**

"Man alone possesses the single quality that gives meaning and purpose to G-d's creation. Without man, the universe is a mere machine. Every mineral, plant and animal behaves in accordance with an ironclad set of laws dictated by its inborn nature, and has neither the inclination nor the ability to behave otherwise. **Only man reflects his Creator in that he possesses free**

choice; only man can, will and act contrary to his nature; only man can make of himself something other than what he is, transcending the very parameters of the self into which he was born. So, only man's deeds have true significance." These are some of the most profound words I read during the Jewish New Year or Rosh Hashanah, the day that emphasizes the centrality of man in creation.

The Torah portion of Pinchas (Pinhas) teaches us that the land of Israel was divided by lottery. A similar lottery is administered to the soul before leaving heaven and coming down to this world. Each soul is paired with a particular ***parcel of land***, a unique destiny, ***a lot in life***. "Our soul is on a divine mission and we all have a unique destiny to fulfill- to settle and develop a particular *parcel of land* with acts of goodness and kindness. Sometimes when we hit rough spots in our lives, (like what I experienced???) we may lose faith in the lottery's divine accuracy. The knowledge that this is a match made in heaven fuels our confidence, commitment and excitement in tackling our portion in life.

Many books and body of work such as Eckhart Tolle's "*The Power of Now*", the Dalai Lama's teachings, meditations and other attempts at exploring healing of the mind, body and soul and ways to reach *enlightenment* is proliferating everywhere. Their popularity is soaring and I have observed that themes of guides to inner life and finding life's meaning comes your way by expanding your mind and not by narrowing it. They all can be deciphered in the teachings of the Torah and I can't help but wonder if Eckhart Tolle read Chaim Miller's[67] books and understood *kabbalah* that he would gladly incorporate those in his book as he had included the teachings of *Jesus* and *Buddha*.

On the other hand, **kabbalah**, (which means to receive, Jewish *esoterism*) offers a bold transformation of the scriptural understanding of God and the universe. Rabbi Chaim Miller[66] briefly discussed that in *kabbalah*, ethical and ritual deeds are perceived as having a strikingly different role. *God and the world are linked in a causal system.* Through the correct actions and intentions, we somehow *activate* the Godhead, harmonize Divine emanations, and cause them to flow into the world, bringing the desired positive results. To stress that it is not the figment of human imagination, but was actually received from a higher source is being explored and is flourishing and I have only read a limited amount of information about *kabbalah* and they already fascinate me and I want more….

There are many Jews who were lost and confused in their spirituality and searched enlightenment through Buddhism or even Atheism before rediscovering the beauty of Judaism as Rabbi Carlebach[68] had observed especially during the 1960's generation of *free love.* Sometimes, man wanders around for so long that we don't see the trees from the forest.

Parsha **"Bere'shit"** which means **"in the beginning"** provides us with so many insights. As Rabbi Chaim Miller clearly summarized from the Jerusalem Talmud; **Bereshit, the first parsha** starts with Bet which is the first letter of the word **Berakha** "blessing" instead of **alef** which is the first letter of the word **arur** which means "curse." The Torah's foundation as he has illuminated is the belief that *"God created the universe. You can experience creation contemplating the fact that God recreates the world to keep us in existence for the purpose of sanctifying the mundane, making a home for Him down below"*. Every day, God says to us "where are you?" – how are you using your capabilities and talents to make the world a better place? (3.9)". The indispensable value and significance of *time* is further emphasized with this phrase; **"God *finished working exactly as the Sabbath began*"**. (2.2). Every single moment is important and you should endeavor to not misuse or waste even a second.

For several years, I contemplated, self- introspected and a few years ago, realized I did not need to oppose what is my destiny. The *Torah* is a powerful tool of personal transformation, reading the **Tanya** helps me calm the worries of my body, mind heart and soul and I am in awe of discovering answers to my quests especially on matters that perplexes me (and I am just at the beginning of this journey, now I know why Yeshiva boys ponder on Jewish texts late into the night !).

In her article reflecting on the holiday of Purim, Ms. Yocheved Sidof[69], Executive Director of Lamplighters *Yeshivah*, stated that Jewish women attempt to simultaneously remain hidden and yet stay visible. We blend in as Jews and maintain our silence; our anonymity. Perhaps we need to beckon one another as Mordechai did to Esther, and remind each other that we have been put here for a purpose that does not allow us to hide. We too must dare to make ourselves visible as Jews. The world, our fellow Jews and G-d need us! When we are rooted in a mission that needs us, our visibility is warranted but it comes with responsibility and vulnerability; we have to have the courage to take risks".

I am delighted to have given the Torah a chance to enlighten me and guide my path to a more purposeful life, find meaning in my personal transformation, experience real joy, gratitude and awe in the rituals that others find "ancient, restrictive, not 21st century America or irrelevant for the age of information technology or even for future generations". The teachings are timeless and give profound relevance to my existence, quiets my restless soul and infuses me with wisdom and a sense of gratitude that even the challenges in my life I now perceive as blessings thru the insights and lessons I have learned.

I have embraced the education and moral values derived from the Torah and Jewish life to help me reach my full potential, respect life, tackle the learning curves and make use of my talents to its maximum. I aim to do daily acts of love, kindness and compassion and inspire others to do the same; contribute to humanity; make this world a more meaningful and better place to live and pay gratitude to G-d the almighty of what is apportioned to me. May *Hashem* guide me in all my current and future endeavors and usher me to my ultimate **tikkun olam** as well as yours. (*A Jewish concept defined by acts of kindness performed to perfect or repair the world*).

AM YSRAEL CHAI ! (The nation of Israel lives).

APPENDIX

Books I have Read in my Journey to a Meaningful and Joyful Jewish Life

1. TORAH: The Five Books of Moses: compiled by Rabbi Chaim Miller, Brooklyn, NY: Lifestyle Books. First Edition © 2011.
2. Bringing Heaven Down to Earth: Book by Menachem Mendel Schneerson. Edited by Tzvi Freeman. CreateSpace Independent Publishing Platform, Dec. 14, 2011.
3. The Bamboo Cradle: Avraham Schwartzbaum; Feldheim, January 1, 1988.
4. Strangers to the Tribe: Portraits of Interfaith Marriage -Gabrielle Glaser, Houghton Mifflin, 1997.
5. The Chosen: Author: Chaim Potok, Fawcett, April 12, 1987.
6. Turning Judaism Outward: A Biography of the Rebbe, Menachem Mendel Schneerson, O.B.M., ©2014 by Chaim Miller, First Edition. New York: Kol Menachem.
7. Man's Search for Meaning- Frankl, Viktor. Touchstone edition. Shimon and Shuster. © 1984.
8. Night: Elie Wiesel, Bantam Books. ©1982.

9. The Diary of a Young Girl: Anne Frank. Bantam edition, © 1993.
10. Toward a Meaningful Life: Simon Jacobson. Perennial Currents (Harper Collins Publishers) © 2002.

WORKS CITED

[1] Fiddler on the Roof. Wikipedia.org; *L' Chaim! 50 Facts About Fiddler on the Roof on the Musical's 50th Anniversary*. Broadway.com

[2] Pesach Observance. What is Passover? Chabad.org.

[3] Rabbi Ismar Schorch, Chancellor of the Jewish Theological Seminary. *Easter and Passover* in My Jewish Learning.com

[4] The Virtual Jewish History Tour: Philippines. The Jewish Virtual Library.org

[5] Pannack, Laura. LauraPannack.com and worldpressphoto.org

[6] Benton, Maya. "Portrait of Orthodox Girl in Synagogue Wins International Photography Award" In *Tablet*, *The Scroll*. November 14, 2014.

[7] Orthodox – Jews.com "Everything you need to know about Orthodox Jews".

[8] Kosher or Kashrut dietary rules . Chabad.org and Aish.com

[9] Escape from Sobibor (TV Movie 1987) IMDb Movies and Wikipedia.org

[10] Chanukah- Hanukkah . What is Hanukkah? –Chabad.org

[11] Yutopia- The Online Home of Rabbi Josh Yuter: The Meaning of "Bashert" in Rabbinic Judaism and its Implications. joshyuter.com

[12] Christmas in the Philippines "Media Noche- a lavish midnight feast" Wikipedia.org

[13] Rabbi Louis Jacobs, "The World to Come" My Jewish Learning.com

[14] Rabbi Noson Weisz. The Book of Ruth: A Mystery Unraveled- Aish.org. Ruth. May 14, 2002

[15] Maimonides, (Moseh ben Maimon or Rambam). Wikipedia.org; The Jewish Encyclopedia.

[16] Rabbi Miller, Chaim, "Turning Judaism Outward" – a biography of the Rebbe Menachem Mendel Schneerson O.B.M., ©2014 by Chaim Miller, First Edition, New York: Kol Menachem, pages 331-333

[17] Rabbi Aaron Moss "Why is Jewishness Passed Down Through the Mother?". Chabad.org

[18] Jewish New Year or "Rosh Hoshana". Aish.com

[19] Baal Teshuvah, The (lit "master of return"), Chabad.org; My Jewish Learning

[20] Wahrman, Miryam Z. Kidney Donor, "My children should see what it means to be a Jew"; Jewish Standard ; August 28, 2009.

[21] Rabbi Moshe Weissman, *The Little Midrash Says: MY FIRST PARHSA READER* © 1986 (Brooklyn, New York: Bnay Yakov Publications).

[22] TORAH: The Five Books of Moses, compiled by Rabbi Chaim Miller; "Parsha Lec Lecha", First Edition © 2011 by Chaim Miller (Brooklyn, NY: Lifestyle Books) pp.62-86.

[23] Kenny, Glenn, "Brooklyn" Movie review @ Roger Ebert.com . November 4, 2015

[24] Tauber, Yanki. The Scroll . Chabad.org

[25] Popova, Maria. "Eli Wiesel's Timely Nobel Peace Prize Acceptance Speech on Human Rights and Our Shared Duty in Ending Injustice. Brainpickings.org

[26] TORAH: The Five Books of Moses: compiled by Rabbi Chaim Miller, "Parsha Balak" First Edition © 2011 by Chaim Miller (Brooklyn, NY: Lifestyle Books) p.954.

[27] Sheldon, Christie Marie; "Love or Above Program", www.unlimitedabundance.com

[28] Frank, Annelies Marie; Author "The Diary of A Young Girl (1942-1944)." Anne Frank Center for Mutual Respect.

[29] Dan Senor and Saul Singer. *Start -Up Nation: The Story of Israel's Economic Miracle.* New York: Hachette Book Group, 2009.

[30] Gill, Alan H. Op- Ed*: In its time of need, repaying a debt to the Philippine*s in the Jewish Telegraphic Agency. Nov. 12, 2013.

[31] Rabbi Noah Weinberg. "Shabbat- Heaven on Earth". In Aish Ha Torah, Aish.com.

[32] Miller, Rabbi Chaim. TORAH: *The Five Books of Moses.* Brooklyn, New York: Lifestyle Books, 2011.

[33] Rabbi Posner, Menachem "What is Shabbat ?" Chabad.org

[34] Mendel Hurwitz Prepares to Become a Man- Video. Oprah.com

[35] Miller, Chaim, The Rebbe's Army in *Turning Judaism Outward* (Brooklyn: Kol Menachem, 2014) pages 337- 357.

[36] Rabbi Yossy Goldman. Parshah: Mishpatim. *Is Religion Still Relevant?* www. Chabad.org

[37] Brooks, David. Opinion: "How Covenants Make Us," The New York Times, April 5, 2016.

[38] Newman, Marissa. *The 10 most anti-Semitic countries and the 10 least anti-Semitic, according to a new global ADL survey.* The Times of Israel, May 13, 2014.

[39] TORAH: The Five Books of Moses: compiled by Rabbi Chaim Miller, "Parsha Shemini" First Edition © 2011 by Chaim Miller (Brooklyn, NY: Lifestyle Books) pages 638-658.

[40] Veith, Walter, PhD. The Science Behind Biblical Clean and Unclean Foods. You Tube- Sept.3, 2014.

[41] Benhamou, Rebecca, "French bestseller unravels Nazi propagandist's cryptic last words about Purim", In *The Times of Israel*, Dec. 2012.

[42] Holzkenner, Rochel " 5 Things I Learned About Being a Woman From Visiting the Mikvah "- Chabad.org

[43] Schusterman, Chana Rachel, Counting the Omer (video) . *The Kabbalah of Self- Refinement* .Chabad.org

[44] International Academy of Orthokeratology; http://www.orthokacademy.com.

[45] Sacks, Rabbi Jonathan, *Teshuvah, Tefilla and Tzedakah* : Chabad.org.

[46] Kumer, Dinka. *What is Tashlich?* Chabad.org

[47] Yellin, Deena, " A Jewish Boy's First Haircut". Chabad.org

[48] Money Dance- Weddings in the Philippines: weddingsinthephilippines.com, Nov. 26, 2012.

[49] Scheib, Ariel . *Philippines Virtual Jewish History Tour.* Jewish Virtual Library. jsource

[50] Tracing the Tribe: *The Jewish Genealogy Blog .Philippines: Israel and a much older connection.* Tracingthetribe.blogspot.com

[51] Philippines Jewish Community. Jewish times Asia.org

[52] Park, Madison. *How the Philippines Saved 1,200 Jews during the Holocaust*, CNN Live TV. Feb. 3,2005.

[53] Smith, Dinitia. *Herbert Zipper, 92, Founder of Secret Orchestra at Dachau- The New York Times.* April 23, 1997

[54] Paulo Alcazaren . *Loving the Zippers* in CITY SENSE. Updated January 21, 2012.

[55] Chris Pasles, *Colburn Dance Institute gets $9-million donation.* Los Angeles Times. June 21, 2008.

[56] Goldman, Bruce. *Cigar Saviors: The Frieder Brothers* in Cigar Aficionado, posted March 7,2005.

[57] Ephraim, Frank. *Escape to Manila: From Nazi Tyranny to Japanese Terror.* University of Illinois Press, Oct. 1, 2010.

[58] Filipinos *gave an open door to European Jews fleeing Hitler and his Nazis,* in the Manila Times, August 24, 2014.

[59] Izon, Noel and Delmendo, Sharon. *An Open Door: Jewish Rescue in the Philippines.* (Extended Trailer). Youtube.com.

[60] Villareal, Melo. *PHIL EXCEL Art Center inaugurates Jack Nasser Collection* in Out of Town blog. www.outoftownblog.com. March 30, 2016

[61] Dumaual, Mario " Mike Hanopol to become first Filipino rabbi" ABS-CBN News and Current Affairs. May 12, 2015

[62] Weinstein, Miriam, "The Surprising Power of Family Meals: *How Eating Together Makes Us Smarter, Stronger, Healthier and Happier. Hanover,* NH: Steerforth Press L.C., ppl-2.

[63] Serby, Steve, *American Pharoah's jockey's divine inspiration for Triple Crown* . New York Post. June 4, 2015.

[64] Drape, Joe. *American Pharoah Wins Belmont Stakes and Triple Crown.* The New York Times. June 5, 2015.

[65] Olidort, Baila, editorial July/ Aug. 2015, Lubavitch International. www.Lubavitch.com

[66] Frankl, Viktor. Man's Search for Meaning, Touchstone edition © 1984. Shimon and Shuster.

[67] Miller, Rabbi Chaim. TORAH: *The Five Books of Moses.* Brooklyn, New York: Lifestyle Books, 2011.

[68] Mandelbaum, Yitta Halberstam: Holy Brother: *Inspiring Stories and Enchanted Tales about Rabi Shlomo Carlebach,* Jason Aronson, Nov.30, 2002.

[69] Sidof, Yocheved. *Losing Anonymity,* Lubavitch International publication, p.6. www.Lubavitch.com

AUTHOR BIOGRAPHY

BELEN (HEBREW NAME: **CHAYA**) LORETO Grand is an Advanced Registered Nurse Practitioner who converted to Judaism in 2004. She loves to attend and host Shabbat dinners and welcomes you to her "Jewish home". Her quest is to spread love, kindness, forgiveness and compassion in the world. To envision a planet made up of nations waging **peace** with each other.

Her goal is to establish centers for Judaic studies at universities in the Philippines where the **7 Noahide Laws** will be disseminated in collaboration with CHABAD emissaries.

www.ingramcontent.com/pod-product-compliance
Lightning Source LLC
LaVergne TN
LVHW011230080426
835509LV00005B/417